"Schultze and Badzinski have written a primer on what it means to take interpersonal communication seriously from a Christian perspective. In eight brief chapters, the authors cover many of the common topics of their subfield from an explicitly Christian worldview. Moreover, they integrate issues, questions, and problems from the realm of social media—Facebook, Twitter, Instagram—and relate those communicative media to such thorny interpersonal issues as forgiveness, cultural difference, reconciliation, peacemaking, evaluation of self and others, conflict avoidance, and truthtelling. In the end, knowing the truth as God has revealed it in his Word, through his Son, and in his creation is the standard against which all communication is measured."

—**Martin J. Medhurst**, Baylor University

"*An Essential Guide to Interpersonal Communication* will shake up your vision for relating. Professors Schultze and Badzinski understand that relating starts with the Spirit's virtues, such as gratitude and responsibility, which lead us to the redemptive skills of listening well, forgiving, and encouraging others. Along the way they point out our need to be true and to aim for peace while letting go of the myth that we can control everything about our relationships. Recommended for personal reflection and college classroom learning in communication and psychology."

—**Bill Strom**, Trinity Western University; author
of *The Relationship Project: Moving from "You and Me" to "We"*

"This is not your ordinary interpersonal text. Schultze and Badzinski uniquely combine communication theory and practice with centuries of spiritual wisdom, resulting in an engaging, practical, highly accessible guide that can be used as a stand-alone text or in conjunction with others. I highly recommend Schultze and Badzinski's *Essential Guide* for use in universities, churches, or any other setting where authentic, life-giving communication is desired."

—**Mary Albert Darling**, Spring Arbor University

"In *An Essential Guide to Interpersonal Communication*, Quentin Schultze and Diane Badzinski present students and others interested in healthy relationships with a wonderful companion to guide their reflection on and self-understanding of this important area. The balance between biblical sources and academic research sets this book apart from others and will make it valuable not only in schools but in church settings as well. Schultze and Badzinski do a brilliant job of capturing the eight key elements of healthy interpersonal relationships."

—**Paul A. Soukup, SJ**, Santa Clara University; author of *Out of Eden: 7 Ways God Restores Blocked Communication*

"Rarely does brilliance sing; but wisdom is poetic in Proverbs and Augustine, and in this phosphorescent book for the Twitter age. With its readability index a perfect ten, this book by award-winning authors turns the pivotal ideas of interpersonal communication into pathways of harmony and transformation."

—**Clifford Christians**, University of Illinois

"This book is accessible, practical, and inspirational and avoids meaningless generalities. It is filled with relevant examples and plentiful quotes. I know of no higher compliment than to say, 'It made me think.'"

—**G. L. Forward**, Point Loma Nazarene University

AN ESSENTIAL *Guide to* Interpersonal Communication

BUILDING GREAT RELATIONSHIPS
with FAITH, SKILL, AND VIRTUE *in the*
AGE *of* SOCIAL MEDIA

QUENTIN J. SCHULTZE
and DIANE M. BADZINSKI

B
Baker Academic
a division of Baker Publishing Group
Grand Rapids, Michigan

Published by Baker Academic
a division of Baker Publishing Group
P.O. Box 6287, Grand Rapids, MI 49516-6287
www.bakeracademic.com

Printed in the United States of America

Library of Congress Cataloging-in-Publication Data
Schultze, Quentin J. (Quentin James), 1952–
    An essential guide to interpersonal communication : building great
relationships with faith, skill, and virtue in the age of social media / Quentin J.
Schultze and Diane M. Badzinski.
        pages cm
    Includes bibliographical references and index.
    ISBN 978-0-8010-3894-5 (pbk.)
    1. Interpersonal communication—Religious aspects—Christianity. 2. Social
media—Religious aspects—Christianity. 3. Interpersonal relations—Religious
aspects—Christianity. I. Title.
BV4597.53.C64S38 2015
248.4—dc23
                                                                    2015016405

15 16 17 18 19 20 21   7 6 5 4 3 2 1

Contents

Acknowledgments

While working on this book for five years, we piled up so many debts to so many people that we hardly know where to begin acknowledging them. Probably the place to start is with our students at Colorado Christian University, Calvin College, and Spring Arbor University. They were our first and best audience for trying out our ideas. They also kept our minds on the intended audience for the book, helping us avoid language that was overly academic or unengaging. Thanks to all of them for encouraging us as teachers as well as scholar-writers.

Colleagues and friends reviewed various versions of the manuscript and gave us remarkably good advice. In fact, we rewrote the manuscript significantly because of the time they dedicated to serving our readers and us. These dedicated souls include Robert Woods, Bill Strom, Paul Soukup, Em Griffin, G. L. Forward, Tim Muehlhoff, Stephanie Bennett, and Ron Welch.

Calvin College provided one of us (Quentin Schultze) with a sabbatical leave to work on this book. Without that support, we would still be struggling to find time for conducting last-minute research on social media and actually writing the manuscript.

We're grateful for Baker Publishing Group's enthusiastic support for this project. Bob Hosack moved our proposal through the review process at record speed. Arika Theule-Van Dam masterfully edited the manuscript with the help of her colleague Gisèle Mix. Paula

Gibson's art team did a terrific job; we liked the cover immediately. Kara Day, Bryan Dyer, Mason Slater, and the rest of the marketing team were helpful and effective throughout the process. Baker was a joy to work with. Thanks to all.

Our spouses and children sometimes got the short end of the stick as we worked evenings and weekends. We greatly appreciate their understanding and love.

Introduction

We wrote this book for everyone who wants to enjoy great relationships in our technological age. We wrote it for people of faith who desire relationships that are a taste of heaven on earth.

New communication technologies come and go, but the essentials of great communication never change. Today communication students often are introduced to the ancient art of *rhetoric* (persuasion) but rarely hear about the communication-related wisdom in, for instance, the Old Testament book of Proverbs or the New Testament book of James. Throughout history, theologians developed profound biblical insights about human communication that can be applied even to the newest communication technologies.

Consider this age-old saying attributed to medieval monks: "Speak only if you can improve upon the silence." (Possible interpretations: "God has already spoken. Can you do better?" or "Don't be a fool by putting your foot in your mouth.") This saying addresses the wisdom of listening and the importance of silence. Today we might say, "Text a message only if you can improve upon a blank screen."

Also ponder this adage, credited to St. Augustine of Hippo: "A Christian should be an alleluia from head to toe." (Possible interpretation: "Be grateful to God, and let your gratitude shape everything you do, including all communication in all media.")

We have written this book to help people practice the enduring essentials of interpersonal communication in the age of social media and through the lens of Christian wisdom. Our book is a practical and inspiring guide for being a faithful as well as an effective communicator in today's multimedia world.

The two of us are communication scholars and teachers. We use high-tech and high-touch media. We love reading good books, so we aimed to write one that others would delight in reading and discussing.

Although we are both Christians, we realize along with St. Augustine that all truth is God's truth. One doesn't have to be a Christian or even religious to discover great principles about communicating well. Social science has taught the two of us a lot about interpersonal communication, especially in the last thirty years; we share some of those findings in this book, especially recent research on the impact of social media on relationships. Given our faith commitments, however, we are especially attuned to how Christian Scripture and theology reveal the essentials of great interpersonal communication. We wrote this book primarily as a supplemental or stand-alone text for use in Christian colleges, universities, seminaries, and churches.

A key word in each chapter title—such as "listen" and "peace"— refers to a concept in the field of interpersonal communication. Also, we italicize key terms throughout the book and provide a definition within the same or a nearby sentence. The chapters build consecutively upon each other. We start with "Be Grateful," which shows that communicators' attitudes fundamentally shape how they perceive and treat others. From a Christian perspective, the foundational attitude for communication is gratitude.

In the second chapter, "Listen Attentively," we discuss the importance of listening, which is paying attention to reality through all of the available media. As we become better listeners, we get to know others more personally, sometimes even intimately. But we live in such noisy, high-traffic times—filled with video, audio, and text—that it can be difficult to stay focused. Listening helps transform the chaotic messaging of everyday life into rewarding friendships.

In chapter 3, "Single-Task," we explain why multitasking is not usually compatible with great interpersonal communication. The newest, fastest communication technologies will not necessarily improve our communication. Too often, high-tech communication distracts us rather than connects us to others; every message alert seems equally worthy of our attention and prevents us from fully engaging with other individuals and groups.

In the fourth chapter, "Know Yourself," we explain how important it is for us to know both our self-identities and our social identities. Often our self-identities—our views of ourselves—are distorted. After all, when we look into a mirror or snap a photo of ourselves, we want to make ourselves look good. That's not all bad. But our real self-identities are not so neat and clean. Image-editing software like Photoshop can't erase our two relationship-robbing tendencies: (1) to hide from others (we call it *cocooning*) and (2) to put down others (we call it *criticizing*). These practices then negatively affect our social identities—how others view us.

In chapter 5, "Relate Openly," we look at the importance of being truthful and true to one another. Authentic persons say what they mean and mean what they say. *Self-disclosure* (revealing what we really think or feel) can be risky since others might be critical of us or even reject us. But if we lie, we reduce others' trust in us. From a Christian perspective, authenticity is a kind of mutual faithfulness in which each party knows "where" the other person truly is in the relationship.

In chapter 6, "Encourage Others," we address a profoundly important type of interpersonal communication: encouragement. In order to flourish in relationships we need both inner resources, like self-motivation, and outer resources, such as heartening words from friends, family, and God. In Scripture, encouragement is one of the most frequently used means of building people up and helping them avoid *discouragement* (a lack of courage to go on in the face of past or feared disappointment). One of the blessings of social media is that they can provide additional ways for us to disclose our discouragement and offer others encouragement.

In chapter 7, "Promote Peace," we look at the inevitable conflict that arises in relationships and suggest a biblical model for peace based on the Hebrew ideal of *shalom*—justice and peace based on right relations. After revealing myths about interpersonal conflicts—such as the myth that verbal conflict is far less relationally significant than physical conflict—we describe biblical peace as lives that are rich with community and hope rather than just with the absence of negative conflicts. By living well relationally with the help of the Spirit, people can flourish together in peace, pointing each other toward the new heaven and new earth that God is preparing for the eternal kingdom.

In the last chapter before the conclusion, "Restore Relationships," we explore how we can faithfully address broken relationships. Of course God's forgiveness is at the heart of the gospel. So this chapter explores how and when to practice forgiveness, recognizing that rebuilding some torn-apart relationships is not easy and requires plenty of patience and grace.

In the concluding chapter we return to the topic of gratitude, calling for a kind of celebration of relationships in the age of social media. We suggest that older and newer media—from speaking to texting—are all signs of the "opening up" of creation, designed to equip us with the means to experience greater joy and delight. When it comes to interpersonal communication, there are not good and bad media. Instead, God offers us an expanding array of media so that we can discover and enjoy the most fitting media for particular situations. *Fittingness*—or "appropriateness"—ought to be our guide in everyday interpersonal discourse. One interesting implication of our perspective is that we need to make sure we don't lose some older "media" of communication—such as engaging in mealtime conversation, walking and hiking, playing board games, and taking vacations with family or road trips with friends—that can still play a fitting role in building great relationships. We offer a balanced perspective with plenty of hope and encouragement.

Practicing communication well is essential because it fosters humans' three main types of relationships: our relationships with God, with others (our biblical "neighbors"), and with ourselves. As we show across these chapters, mastering interpersonal communication is all about nurturing those three relationships simultaneously through appropriate media.

Finally, we indicate throughout the book that the quality of human relationships depends on a combination of *faith* (whom we trust and follow), *skill* (how we interact with God, others, and ourselves), and *virtue* (the qualities of our character—or the habits of our heart).

By focusing in this book on all three—faith, skill, and virtue—we show how to flourish in life-giving relationships filled with joy and delight. Even more than that, we offer samples from the kingdom feast that is already being prepared for us but seems missing in the noisy networks of everyday life.

So what really distinguishes our vision for interpersonal communication from that of other books is the God-given potential in human beings to overcome their selfish tendencies and to form life-giving relationships filled with joy and delight. People's hard work along with God's surprising grace can transform everyone's relationships into heavenly signs of hope. We hope that all readers will begin to flourish anew as they discover what God has in store for their relationships.

One of the communication professors who read an early manuscript of this book was moved to reach out in love to an estranged sibling. They had not spoken for years as resentments had piled up in their heads. Then one kind, inviting email turned that relationship around. Soon the siblings, living in different parts of the country, met in person with plenty of hugs and kisses. It was the first time in twenty-five years that the siblings and parents had shared a meal together. This is how God renews our relationships—one message at a time. And one book at a time. May this book continue to sow seeds of relational renewal for many more people, so that they can flourish like flowers on a warm spring morning.

Thanks for listening.

1

BE GRATEFUL

In a live television interview, comedian Louis C. K. said that in today's technological world "everything's amazing and nobody's happy." He joked that airline passengers complain about having to wait on runways. "Oh really, well what happened next? Did you fly through the air incredibly, like a bird? Did you partake in the miracle of human flight? . . . Everybody on every plane should just constantly be going 'OH . . . WOW.' You're sitting in a chair in the sky."[1]

We all take much for granted. And we quickly complain when we're inconvenienced by something as insignificant as a slow internet connection or a dropped cell call.

Yet one of the most amazing gifts we take for granted is our ability to communicate. Human communication isn't just about sending and receiving messages. It's about sharing our lives. It's about friendship rather than loneliness. It's about flourishing in community, including *interpersonal* (person-to-person) relationships with family and friends.

In this chapter we look at the most important attitude that should shape all of our communication: gratitude. Great interpersonal communication begins and ends with gratitude, which flows from a grateful heart. We should give thanks for the gift of communication, for having other people to relate to, for being able to commune especially with God, and for all of those who led the way for us by teaching and modeling grateful communication. Without the gift of communication we would have no relationships and therefore no community life. By God's grace, made in his image, we possess a phenomenal capacity to build great relationships. This is why the most important attitude is exactly what Louis C. K. bantered about—gratitude.

Being Grateful

Heartfelt gratitude is the best way to begin communicating with others. This includes gratitude for the gift giver (God), for those we communicate with, and for the gift of communication that equips us to relate to others. We should rightly give thanks for people such as family and teachers who taught us about communication and modeled it for us, and for the people who created the communication technologies we depend on daily. Louis C. K. rightly gave thanks for the miracle of flight, but he could have just as appropriately given thanks to the people who invented the technology and the professionals who serve the airline.

Heartfelt gratitude naturally leads us to be less selfish and more servant-oriented. When we accept our own communicative ability as a gift from God and then desire in our hearts to use the gift to love and serve others, we are well on our way to becoming faithful interpersonal communicators. Spiritual theologian James M. Houston writes, "The heart is the source of all the attitudes that go to make up a person."[2] Our hearts form our character and direct our communication.

Priest Thomas á Kempis copied the Bible by hand no fewer than four times before writing *The Imitation of Christ*, probably the most popular Christian book of all time except for the Bible. He says, "A wise lover considers not so much the lover's gift as the giver's love."[3] He adds, "A barrage of words does not make the soul happy, but a pure conscience generates a bountiful confidence in God."[4] The more we honestly love God, the more our words will help us love others and ourselves. "A true Christian," writes Scottish theologian John Baillie, "is one who never for a moment forgets what God has done for him in Christ, and whose whole comportment and whole activity have their roots in the sentiment of gratitude."[5]

Modeling the Right Attitude

Our hearts can hold three basic attitudes toward others: displeasure, indifference, and gratitude. These shape how we communicate with one another and especially how others perceive us.

Displeased communicators tire us with complaints and criticisms. Their hearts say to others, "You don't live up to my standards" and "I'm better than you are." We generally avoid such people unless we're likewise discontented persons. Negative people attract one another. Grumblers gather to commiserate. Louis C. K. reminds us how easily we grumble about inconveniences while forgetting the underlying miracles.

Indifferent communicators wear us out with apathy and inertia. Their hearts say to others, "Whatever." It's hard to get to know such people well because they don't work at developing close relationships. They live superficially.

SIX TYPES OF COMMUNICATORS FOR WHICH TO GIVE THANKS

1. Encouragers—who build us up
2. Advocates—who speak up on our behalf
3. Listeners—who care about our thoughts and feelings
4. Storytellers—who give us joy and delight
5. Forgivers—who make things right when we're wrong
6. Challengers—who ask appropriate questions about our communication

---

Grateful communicators welcome us into their lives, encourage us, and direct us toward affirming relationships. Their warm hearts say to others, "You are a gift. I care about you." We naturally want to care about them in return.

Grateful communicators in every medium speak appreciatively. They avoid language that reflects ingratitude or indifference, such as "whatever," "who cares," and "so what." Instead, they look for opportunities to compliment others and to remind them how much they are valued, even for the "little things." Often one or two words of genuine gratitude will make another person's day. "Thanks for your kind words." "I appreciate the way you listen to me." "Your encouragement means a lot to me." Even a simple text message of thanks can bless the recipient.

Ungrateful communicators, on the other hand, spread complaints through their networks of friends and family. The people of Israel grumbled against the very God who delivered them from Egypt.[6] They griped about God's seemingly lousy leadership. They complained about inadequate provisions. They questioned God's presence and power.[7] The exodus story links the Israelites' murmurings against God with their failure to remain faithful.[8]

Our gratitude begins evaporating when we overlook God's grace and start groaning about our circumstances and criticizing others. We may find temporary joy in putting down others and grumbling about God, but such a lousy attitude will squelch our ability to form joy-filled, lasting relationships.

Embracing Thankfulness

In the Hebrew and Christian traditions, real appreciation is a life-shaping attitude that grows in our hearts as we praise God *in* all things and give thanks to God *for* all good things. Believing in God is one thing. Being wholeheartedly grateful to God is much more. As the writer of Proverbs puts it, such gratefulness leads us to write mercy and truth "on the tablet of [our] heart."[9] Rabbi Abraham Heschel, a leading Jewish theologian of the twentieth century, says, "The truth of being human is gratitude; its secret is appreciation."[10]

Can we truly communicate out of love for others if we lack appreciativeness? Not really. Gratitude is our first blessing, which in turn makes us a blessing to others. It's our emotional home in the presence of God. When we're ungrateful, we lack a loving home and cannot love others.[11] The words "gratitude" and "grace" spring from the same Latin root. God's love-drenched grace inspires us—through the work of the Spirit—to give thanks to God and in return to love others as well as ourselves.

Gratitude leads us away from selfish communication and toward mutually beneficial relationships. Robert Emmons, author of *Thanks!*, says that gratitude "implies humility—a recognition that we could not be who we are or where we are in life without the contributions of others."[12] The highly influential twentieth-century German theologian Karl Barth writes, "God's grace and our gratitude go together like 'heaven on earth.'"[13] The apostle Paul proclaims, "Rejoice always, pray continually, give thanks in all circumstances; for this is God's will for you in Christ Jesus."[14] Gratitude is foundational for relational flourishing.

Communication skills are important but insufficient for strong interpersonal relationships. Without gratitude, our interpersonal communication tends to deform our relationships. We expect from others far more than we offer them. Acclaimed Christian philosopher Alvin Plantinga says, "The initial difference between believer and demon is a matter of affections: the former is inspired to gratitude and love, the latter to fear, hatred, and contempt."[15] Generally speaking, religiously and spiritually engaged people are more grateful people.[16] Grateful people, in turn, are more likely to engage in religious and spiritual activities.[17] Our hearts and our relational skills are intimately connected to our faith; our skills spread the messages of our hearts throughout our social networks.

Communing with God

As followers of Jesus Christ, we're never really alone. Even when we talk to ourselves, God is with us, listening and sending the Holy Spirit to motivate, encourage, and console us. Our communication—or communion—with God sets the stage for all of our other relationships.

God is present to serve us even in our inadequate communication and unsatisfactory relationships. God doesn't abandon us even if we've already spent years learning bad communication habits and living in unsatisfying or abusive relationships. God doesn't leave us alone to try to change hearts and habits just by reading self-help books or taking communication workshops. Instead, God invites us to experience his love and thereby to begin experiencing renewed relationships with him and with others—over and over again.

Moreover, we have no idea how much misunderstanding and how many conflicts God has already helped us through. In the last week alone, we've all communicated with many people but probably suffered few emotionally debilitating conflicts. God has been intervening on our behalf all along. God has been making our communication happen through the work of the Spirit. In a sense, God has been sustaining our relationships with friends, family, and colleagues in spite of our inadequacies.

In other words, the burden for our own interpersonal communication never rests solely on our own shoulders. We share it with the Creator God who gave us the gift of communication and who through the Spirit keeps inviting us into relationships with Jesus and other people (our biblical "neighbors"). All of our successful communication with everyone is a gift from God. God's grace makes it happen. The wonderfully gifted fiction writer Flannery O'Connor, who struggled to learn how to pray, observes, "All of my requests seem to melt down to one for grace."[18] With grace comes gratitude.

Responding to God's Grace

In the Gospel of Luke, chapter 17, ten lepers approach Jesus for healing. They yearn to break free from their isolation on the margins of society. Jesus complies, making them whole. But only one of the lepers subsequently thanks his healer. A lone leper, a despised Samaritan, turns back to Jesus, kneels at the Lord's feet, thanks him, and loudly praises him.

Thus begins a new relationship between God and a child of God, and soon between that former leper and his growing relationships with other persons. Thus emerges a new heart of gratitude, reflected in words of praise. Thus commences a life of faithful communication. We would do well to imitate the leper's grateful communication.

Struggling to discern if it was God's will for her to give thanks for a disease that hardened her skin and internal organs, Marcia pledged, with brutal honesty, "God, I've never lied to you before and I'm not going to start now. There's no way I can thank you for this life-robbing, painful disease or the fact that I'm not going to see my grandchildren grow up. But I will thank you for the things for which I'm truly grateful."[19] She focused on what she could give thanks for, not just on the personal concerns that could diminish her gratitude and tarnish her relationships.

Most astonishing is Marcia's subsequent journal entry: "One morning as I was thinking of things I was thankful for, without even realizing it I heard myself say, 'God, thank you for this disease that's brought me so much closer to you!'"[20] Marcia courageously communed with God, even in the midst of her life-robbing illness. Faithfully employing the gift of communication, she rediscovered gratitude in grace and faith in gratitude.

Communing in Community

What are human beings for? What's our purpose on earth?

Our greatest calling is to glorify Jesus and enjoy God forever. In other words, we're designed for worshipful living. Our lives are meant to be fragrant offerings to Jesus Christ. We're here to love and serve in life-affirming relationships—in communities—with God, our neighbors, and ourselves. "No man is an island," writes John Donne, a seventeenth-century English poet, lawyer, and priest.[21] The word "communication" stems from the same Latin root as the words "community" and "communion," meaning to share, to have things in common, and to experience fellowship.[22]

In the early church, persecuted believers gathered secretly to celebrate their unity in Christ primarily by "communing" together in the Lord's Supper. Participating in the sacrament became a way of forming a faith community. Each believer was an individual who shared with others a common faith in God. Similarly, each of us maintains our own God-given uniqueness even as we share our lives with others. Like each person in the Trinity—Father, Son, and Holy Spirit—every human being is a separate person united in community with other unique persons.

Jackie Turner, age twenty-six, so desired community that she posted an ad on Craigslist asking to rent a family for a holiday—at $8.00 an hour. Although some families invited her to join them for free, she unexpectedly received so many responses from similarly lonely individuals that she decided to start a new family. Rather than renting a family, Turner contacted those who also wanted a home for the holiday and gathered with them to celebrate.[23]

Every one of our interpersonal relationships is grounded in communication and carries the potential for community. Our relationships live in communication. Without communication, they die. Interpersonal communication is all about gratefully nurturing, repairing, and celebrating life-giving relationships. All of our work and play depends on such communication-formed relationships. In a sense, the gift of communication is a love letter from God that invites us into community with the Trinity, one another, and ourselves. This is why our most rewarding interpersonal relationships are a taste of heaven on earth.

Imitating Grateful People

Because communication and community are so intimately connected, we tend to become like the people we spend time with. In other words, our relationships significantly form our own hearts and direct our own words.

So becoming a more faithful, God-serving, neighbor-loving interpersonal communicator requires us to choose our friends wisely. The people we intentionally or unintentionally imitate shape the kind of person we are. To be grateful persons, we need to network with thankful people.

Today we tend to think about interpersonal communication in terms of effective techniques or skills. But also critically important are our *virtues*—our intrinsically good qualities of character. We can't really separate ourselves as persons from our own messages; we are part of the message, not just the messengers. In others' eyes, we are viewed somewhat in terms of our apparent character—not just according to what we literally say, write, or post online.

Moreover, by being virtuous with others we can create nurturing relationships together. As communication scholar Bill Strom puts it in *The Relationship Project*, we learn "virtuous relating."[24]

We learn much about communication from imitation. This is why we need *saintly* (virtuous and faithful) role models that will demonstrate grateful communication. A saintly person acknowledges her or his debt to the cross and is genuinely committed to being Jesus's salt and light in God's world. They are living gratitude. They aim to communicate faithfully, not just skillfully.

Like all other past and present Christians, we're learning daily how to communicate with faith, skill, and virtue. We're figuring out how to be saintly ourselves. We're practicing what it means to be holy rather than just effective communicators. We look to God's Word for guidance. We study the wisdom about communication that we can learn from saints like á Kempis. And we look to the saints in our midst at work, play, home, and worship to show us how to communicate well. In other words, the gift of communication equips us to learn from saintly people how we can be faithful and virtuous as well as skillful communicators.

You will be a far better communicator if you regularly acknowledge and express appreciation to persons who have modeled for you how to communicate gratefully with faith, skill, and virtue. Then ask God to bless them. Consider parents, grandparents, friends, teachers, pastors, coworkers or bosses, and anyone else who served you by demonstrating saintly communication.

Conclusion

Communication skills are essential for building rich and rewarding interpersonal relationships. But first we need the foundation of gratitude because our communication ultimately flows from our hearts. The right attitude is essential. We grow gratitude in our hearts when we network with God and other grateful people. We sour our attitude and tarnish our communication when we tag along with complainers and grumblers.

The more grateful we are, the more deeply we'll love God, neighbor, and self. As author Esther de Waal puts it in a book on spirituality, living gratefully helps us to "see with love and delight, with wonder and tenderness, and above all with gratitude."[25] Comedian Louis C. K. rightly chided his television audience for being ungrateful in the face of so many "miracles" of modern technology. But even more miraculous is the very gift of communication bestowed upon us by a communicating God who invites us into a grateful community with him and others.

In the next chapter we explain what listening is and how to practice it well so that we can offer our grateful hearts to others in service. Listening is how we get to know others as we learn to call them friends, just as Jesus Christ calls us his friends. Only by listening well can we build flourishing relationships.

2

LISTEN ATTENTIVELY

Imagine you are young, single, and available. What would you do if you were attracted to someone? How would you approach that person? Would you schedule a date? If so, where would you go? Why?

Brother Mark Brown, who lives in a monastery near Boston, says that the best relationships are intentional. That's why he spends an hour daily in personal prayer with God. It's also why he uses a dating analogy when he leads church retreats on developing an intimate prayer life. He aims to get participants thinking about forming close relationships. "If you wanted to get to know someone better," he suggests, "you would probably be very intentional. You might even develop some strategies."[1]

The best interpersonal relationships are largely intentional. They grow out of right desire, ample time, and freedom from distractions—especially the "traffic" of everyday life. Above all, they are based on listening, which is the way of focusing on what's important regardless of all the distractions. If we don't listen well to others we'll be lonely, no matter how many connections we have in person or on social media. By listening we get to know others' hopes, joys, and emotional, physical, and spiritual needs. And we can begin to truly appreciate, serve, and even love them. As we explain in this chapter, listening isn't just hearing—it's not even just about sound. First, we explore listening as a necessary but challenging way of attending to reality (to the way things really are) that will challenge many of our assumptions about God, other people, and ourselves. Next, we suggest that listening is essential for choosing relational life rather than relational death. Third, by listening "up" to God and then "out" to others, we can get to know them well enough to have mutually good and deep relationships with them. Fourth, the biblical model for such life-giving relationships is friendships that mirror Jesus Christ's own friendship with us. Finally, the chapter shows that by God's grace we can relate to others with empathy and sympathy.

Challenging Ourselves

Listening isn't easy. Listening is messy. Complicated. Counterintuitive. We can't become good listeners unless we first acknowledge how difficult it is for each of us personally. Novelist Ernest Hemingway puts it squarely: "Most people never listen."[2]

Listening is not just hearing. It's not even just about sound. Listening is attending to reality—to the way things really are with God, others, and us. It's how we pay attention to what is outside of us rather than merely our own internal feelings, desires, and opinions.

Who in your life are truly skilled listeners? How would you know? Here's how: In some ways they probably know you almost as well as you know yourself. They thoughtfully attend and respond to what they perceive as your underlying feelings, not just what you say or text to them. They can tell what you're feeling partly by your nonverbal posturing, especially your facial expressions. They create within you what communication scholar John Shotter calls "a distinct and recognizable feeling of being heard."[3] That's exactly what Brother Mark Brown aims to achieve for people in his workshops on prayer—a real knowledge that God knows, listens, and loves those who turn to him in prayer.

That's not all. These true listeners sympathize and empathize with you. They hold your hand through tough times. They rarely criticize you as a person even when they admonish you for specific misdeeds. They know what hurts and helps you—and aim to aid you. They're not your friends just because it makes them feel good. They're your friends because they accept you for the way you are and yet desire the best for you.

Such *soul-listening* friends are emotionally and spiritually present in your life, possessing an uncanny ability to know what's on your mind and in your heart.[4] One of the first signs of friendship is realizing that you and your friend are opening up to each other's real feelings and not being distracted by all kinds of other issues and messages. That sense of being personally, honestly accepted by another person is emotionally powerful. It echoes Jesus's acceptance of us.

Sometimes couples who have lived together for a lifetime seem to be able to read each other's minds. Their initial dating led them to a rich partnership. Often just how they look at one another is sufficient; they can read the nonverbal nuances—like subtle gestures or eye movements—that tell them what the other person is feeling or thinking. They've reaped the benefits of a lifetime of paying attention to each other.

Real listening is difficult partly because we want reality to conform to our wishes. We're less interested in humbly grasping reality than in avoiding any communication that challenges our assumptions. We even deceive ourselves about ourselves. Just ask a recovering alcoholic, someone hooked on internet pornography, or a compulsive video game player. They try not to listen to themselves because it's too painful. Meanwhile, they are busy selfishly trafficking in messages that make it hard to hear their own hearts.

One of the main tasks of a counselor is to get the counselee to open up. Then the counselor can actively listen to what is really going on in the troubled person's life. Millions of people spend thousands of dollars annually to ensure that they will be listened to confidentially, without fear of being denigrated or rejected.

Many 12-step recovery programs like Alcoholics Anonymous provide a safe place for people to speak and listen to each other talk about their addictions. One way they protect confidentiality is to use only

Five Ways to Avoid Working for a Hellish Boss

Good listening often involves discovering information about people even before we meet them. Yet much of life is a series of "blind dates" with people we know nothing about. This can be extremely important in work contexts. Once we accept a new position, it's too late to decide that we don't want to "date" the boss.

Jessica Dean was very excited to get hired by a hot start-up company developing a new cell phone app—until she found out what her new boss, the owner, was really like: unprofessional, overdemanding, and untrusting. What could she have done to avoid working for "the boss from hell"? She could have listened to the right people to discover reality:

1. Google the boss's name and company to find out more about him.
2. Use LinkedIn to find past employees and interview them about the boss.
3. Ask in the interview how long the job has been open— and why.
4. Ask questions about workplace culture and management style.
5. Observe how the boss seems to interact with others before, during, and immediately after the interview.

Adapted from Dennis Nishi, "How to Spot the Boss from Hell: There Are Ways to Size Up Your Job Interviewer," *Wall Street Journal*, February 8, 2014, http://online.wsj.com/news/articles /SB10001424052702303942404579360784194736714.

each other's first names. By listening to each other's stories of addiction and recovery, participants in these programs receive encouragement, hope, and practical advice. They avoid some of the shame that would accompany telling other people about their personal struggles.

Perhaps texting and social media provide means for beginning relationships in a relaxed way. "Casual, easy, and non-threatening— the simple beauty of text messaging is upending American dating culture," according to *USA Today*. As one thirty-year-old man puts it, "Most of the girls I've hung out with lately prefer a group activity rather than one-on-one." To get positive responses he texts invitations like, "I'm here with a group of people. Show up if you want to." About one-third of males and females say it's less intimidating to ask for a date via text than phone. Does texting make the invitation less personal? One woman says, "Guys are using text messages to send the same message to multiple women. . . . They're kind of fishing for a response."[5]

Texting can help people initially connect, but it can't nurture a deep relationship because it doesn't allow enough opportunity for listening. Couples need to build adequate mutual trust by listening on the phone or by video, and especially in person. Along the way, they need to listen to God, coming to grips personally with God's likely view of their relationship.

Unfortunately, listening to God and to those with whom we're in relationship can be accompanied by a fear of rejection. This fear is partly why so many people pretend that even a miserable relationship will somehow magically improve. It's also why many Christians don't really listen to God. What if we hear something we don't want to face? What if we can't accept ourselves in the light of God's intimate knowledge of everything we think and do? Listening and being listened to can be very sobering. British Chancellor Winston Churchill, who led his nation during World War II, said, "Courage is what it takes to stand up and speak; courage is also what it takes to sit down and listen."[6]

Many people lack the courage to listen to others without scrutinizing them. They're quick to judge and slow to understand. As a result, their friends and family members don't share their real struggles. They all live on the outside of each other, without acknowledging their own, interior persons. They talk. They respond. They live in a high-traffic message environment. But they don't truly listen. Stephen Covey, author of *The Seven Habits of Highly Effective People*, says, "Most people do not listen with the intent to understand; they listen with the intent to reply."[7]

If you'd like to test your listening skills, try talking with several friends about a sermon that you all just heard. Compare first what you think the pastor said. Then compare what the sermon meant to each of you personally—and why. How much of what you heard was what the sermon said, and how much of it was what you wanted to hear?

Listening to good listeners share their stories about listening is critically important for becoming a great listener. Who are the listening saints in your life? You might identify one person who knows you well. List three listening-rich ways that person uses to get to know you—perhaps hanging out, eating or exercising together, asking open-ended questions, or connecting privately with you through social media. Then identify someone you would like to get to know better and use the most appropriate of the three ways to communicate with them. As Brother Mark Brown suggests, relationships require intentionality.

Busyness gets in the way of listening too. If we're hurried and frazzled—and thereby physically, spiritually, or emotionally spent—we can't listen well. Listening requires mental preparedness. As one scholar of listening, Lisbeth Lipari, puts it, real listening takes time, energy, and courage to engage "with what is unfamiliar, strange, and not already understood."[8] Otherwise we live in a series of blind dates, never getting to know others well and never ourselves being known by others. Because we live with so much noise, we have to learn to be intentional about listening. What we need is not more messaging but the kind of solitude that prepares us to be fully present with and perceptively aware of others.[9]

Listening is a critical communication skill for fostering good relationships. There's no shortcut. We can talk incessantly, text up a storm, and post like crazy online. But if there's no mutual, heartfelt listening, we'll feel lonely, neglected, and unsatisfied with life. Online dating sites and other digital ways of connecting are merely tools. They can't guarantee relationships. They can only lead us to people with whom we can begin mutually listening for the sake of a deeper relationship.

We have to choose to become good listeners—and then follow through, step-by-step, day-by-day. In a sense, we're all recovering nonlisteners who need to learn afresh daily what it means to listen. We need a Listeners Anonymous for addicted talkers.

SEVEN SIGNS OF POOR LISTENING

1. Judging others too quickly and harshly
2. Jumping to premature conclusions
3. Responding thoughtlessly
4. Basing opinions of others on first impressions
5. Failing to set aside one's biases and prejudices
6. Seeing reality solely from one's own, limited perspective
7. Focusing on self-centered agendas

Listening for Relational Life over Death

Listening is attending to reality rather than getting caught up in our own narrow, often self-serving view of things. It requires what scholar Ronald C. Arnett and his colleagues call "attentiveness to that which is set before us, rather than that which we might prefer."[10]

When we truly listen to God—often through Christian community—we begin choosing *life* (healthy relationships) over *death* (destructive relationships). Relational death is separation and despair. When we are committed to listening, there is hope for our relationships. When we stop listening—when we cease paying attention to both God and neighbor—our relationships wither and die.

God says to the Israelites after they had wandered from the Lord, "Now what I am commanding you today is not too difficult for you or beyond your reach." He adds that "the word is very near you; it is in your mouth and in your heart so you may obey it." God concludes with the alternatives: "This day I call the heavens and the earth as witnesses against you that I have set before you life and death, blessings and curses. Now choose life, so that you and your children may live and that you may love the LORD your God, listen to his voice, and hold fast to him. For the LORD is your life, and he will give you many years in the land he swore to give to your fathers, Abraham, Isaac and Jacob."[11]

Just like the Israelites, we first have to listen to God to get an accurate picture of reality. Jesus repeatedly calls on those "who have ears" to listen.[12]

God wants us to listen so that we may delight in him, in one another, and in ourselves. Without God, says theologian Ellen T. Charry, we are more likely to "float aimlessly at the mercy of volatile emotions and hormones or be seduced by less worthy companions than the maker of heaven and earth."[13] We can experience soul-satisfying relationships only if we are empowered by the Holy Spirit, drawing upon the same Sprit that enabled Jesus to connect with others.[14] In other words, the quality of our relationships with others depends on the quality of our relationship with God.

When we "listen up" to God before we "listen out" to others, our relationships become richer, deeper, and more satisfying. Life for us becomes a rich life, not just physical existence or temporary happiness. Having attended to God's love for us, we are more willing and able to love others. We've faced God humbly, and we're better equipped to face one another with what the founder of Peacemaker Ministries Ken Sande calls "relational wisdom."

We flourish when, experiencing God's love for us as broken and fearful persons, we rise faithfully to life's challenges, creatively pursue our best passions, and look beyond ourselves so that others too can

Six Skills of "Relational Wisdom"

1. God-awareness—viewing all of life in light of God's truths
2. God-engagement—acting in a way that pleases and honors God
3. Self-awareness—assessing honestly one's emotions, desires, strengths, and weaknesses
4. Self-engagement—mastering one's thoughts and actions to further God's purposes
5. Other-awareness—understanding and empathizing with the experiences of others
6. Other-engagement—working with others in a way that truly benefits them

Adapted from Ken Sande, "Biblical Foundation for Relational Wisdom," Relational Wisdom 360, http://www.rw360.org/biblical-foundation-for-rw/.

find lasting meaning and soul-satisfying relationships.[15] Each time we choose relational life over death we step out of our loneliness and into community with God and neighbor. It's scary. But by first opening up to Jesus, who accepts us unconditionally, we are far more likely to have the courage to open up to others and to listen to others without first judging them.

Outward Listening to Serve Others

Rick and Barb Wise were both twenty-seven years old when they decided to marry. Rick was a virgin—Barb wasn't. Before they could wed, she discovered she was HIV positive. Barb recalled, "I stood paralyzed in disbelief. How could this be? I was in love. I was in love with Rick." Her mind raced ahead, "Would Rick end the relationship?"[16]

Even though Barb's prognosis offered her two weeks to a year to live, she and Rick soon wed. And Barb lived on, for over twenty years and counting. So did their relationship, as they listened to God and to each other in order to discern how to serve one another in such an unusual situation.

The more they listened to God, the more Barb and Rick also listened outwardly to others. They discovered that they could serve others by sharing their own story about the reality of living with HIV/ AIDS. They talked openly about such things as Barb's sexual past and deciding not to have children. They offered a glimpse of what it's like to flourish relationally in difficult circumstances. Grateful to God for every day they would have together, they launched a nonprofit organization to teach others about "forming healthy relationships and hope in marriage."[17]

We too can experience real life in the midst of our broken, challenging relationships. Each of us has a wealth of empathy and love, of joy and delight, waiting to be discovered anew through the gift of listening.

Do you want to be loved and to love others? Then avoid the distractions of everyday life and spend time discovering what's on the minds and in the hearts of your own family, friends, coworkers, and church members. Lipari calls us to be "fully within reach of and open to receive the other," listening "as a kind of hospitality, invitation, a hosting."[18] The alternative is what writer Frederick Buechner describes as living alone, in communion with only ourselves, in a buried life, like a seed in the ground that never germinates to enjoy the sun and the rain, the clouds and the winds.[19] To listen to God and neighbor is to experience life-giving community. Every time you truly pay attention to someone, you honor him or her. Choose friends who will similarly honor you.

God blesses our relationships by granting us openness to him and others. God, as the greatest listener of all, demonstrated—through his own sacrificial love on the cross—that we should be loving servants. As the great biblical commandment puts it, we are to love God and our neighbor as ourselves.[20] We discover how to practice such neighborly love by listening to God and neighbor—by committing to dates with God and neighbor in the midst of our hectic lives.

Flourishing as Friends

The most striking biblical model for such attentive, life-giving relationships is friendship. True friendship is based on mutual respect, understanding, love, and service. By truly listening, we can begin to overcome brokenness, rejection, and loneliness to flourish together as friends.

Broadly speaking, we all live in two types of interpersonal relationships: (1) relatively close relationships of *friendship* and (2) less intimate relationships of *acquaintance*. Friendships are dearer and might include family members, suitemates, romantic partners, coworkers, and other relationships between people who know each other relatively well. Acquaintances include those who do not know each other very well, such as next-door neighbors, members of the broader community, and people we interact with merely in the course of everyday duties like shopping and commuting. At work, for instance, we might know one or two coworkers well enough to call them personal friends, whereas the others are acquaintances whose names we know but whose personal lives we know little about. We'll probably never listen deeply to them—and vice versa.

Our friendships always exist on a spectrum from superficial to deep and mutually self-sacrificing. Your social-media "friends" (really, acquaintances) would probably be interested in the fact that you were jailed for driving recklessly—they might even gossip about it. A good friend would probably bail you out. A truly faithful friend would want to swap places with you in jail if you had to serve time.

For two millennia, flourishing relationally with others has been called friendship. Epicurus, an ancient Greek philosopher, said, "Friendship dances around the world, urging us all toward blessedness."[21] For the ancients, however, friendship was culturally limited, primarily between upper-class males, especially political leaders and philosophers.

In Christianity, friendship took on greater spiritual and egalitarian significance. The North African bishop Augustine of Hippo, followed by the abbot Aelred of Rievaulx, reinterpreted the ancient Greek idea of friendship in the light of Scripture. They viewed friendship as two or three persons participating together in the life of Christ regardless of their social class or gender. Aelred wrote in *Spiritual Friendship* that women and men alike could serve as models of virtue and faith. All believers can thereby exemplify God's loving-kindness.[22]

Jesus names his followers "friends" and calls them to intimacy with himself and each other. He taught that true friends are marked by self-sacrificial love rather than shared social standing.[23] "My command is this: Love each other as I have loved you. Greater love has no one than this: to lay down one's life for one's friends."[24] True friends imitate Christ by using their gifts of communication selflessly to bless each other.

Using the gift of communication to self-sacrificially love one another is ideal Christian friendship. It's a kind of nonsexual or platonic relationship focusing on one another in the midst of fast-paced lives. Such communication equips us to participate in a flourishing community of two or three Christians striving to imitate God's own triune community—to be intimate and mutually sacrificial, working and celebrating together by grace. The Trinity—three persons in one God—is the ultimate model for such friendship. The Trinity is three perfect listeners who know and serve each other intimately, perfectly, and complementarily.

Listening with Empathy and Sympathy

Humans' dual capacities for mutual *empathy* (feeling "with" others) and *sympathy* (feeling "for" others) are at the heart of friendship. These amazing abilities are at the root of our worst and best communication. We can use them both to exploit and to serve others. In the novel *To Kill a Mockingbird*, the father, Atticus, tells his son, "If you can learn a simple trick . . . you'll get along a lot better with all kinds of folks. You never really understand a person until you consider things from his point of view . . . until you climb inside of his skin and walk around in it."[25]

We're created for such sympathy and empathy. They are the opposites of being lonely and self-serving. God says in Genesis that it's wrong for Adam to be alone.[26] In order to flourish, Adam needs a partner, someone with whom he can enjoy life and who has the same communicative abilities, so that together they may be responsible, delighted caretakers of God's world. God creates Eve, a care-giving and care-receiving partner. The two of them can discourse with their Creator and each other. They become the first biblical friends apart from the members of the Trinity (represented in the Christian tradition by God's words, "Let *us* make mankind in *our* image, in *our* likeness"[27]). Before Adam and Eve's disobedience to God, they seemed to be perfectly intersubjective with each other; they could understand each other flawlessly.

SEVEN WAYS TO LISTEN WELL

1. Dedicate yourself—intentionally choose to listen
2. Take time—generously carve out a sufficient period of time
3. Select a location—carefully choose a distraction-free place
4. Focus attention—patiently stay in the moment
5. Be sympathetic—openly accept others' feelings
6. Remain empathetic—nonjudgmentally put yourself in others' shoes
7. Visualize support—genuinely smile and nod

When we choose life over death in our relationships, we aim to follow God's lead with Adam and Eve as soul friends. We seek openness and mutuality with God and others.

Conclusion

From a Christian perspective, human beings are created for particular kinds of relationships, whether online, via phones, or in person. Communication is a means for forming relationships that honor God and demonstrate how we serve one another. *Interpersonal communication*, in particular, is faithfully using the gift of communication to foster shared understanding for life-giving relationships, especially friendships.

When the modern-day monk said that praying is like dating, he tapped into an ancient Hebrew view of communication as relationship building. The gift of communication equips us to grow in communion with God, others, and ourselves. Further, it enables us to form emotionally intimate relationships—friendships—that model sympathy and empathy.

As we show in the next chapter, technology, however, is not always helpful for building such friendships. Newer communication technologies, in particular, speed up the pace and quantity of our messaging, creating ever-more distractions that we have to contend with. Our lives can turn into a series of immediate message alerts if we fail to embrace single-tasking with those with whom we most wish to be friends and perhaps lovers.

3

SINGLE-TASK

James sat in church, struggling to focus on the sermon about Moses reluctantly leading the Israelites from Egyptian bondage to the promised land. James's problem was that people (or was it one person?) kept calling him on his smartphone, which was on vibrate in his zipped jacket pocket.

James thought about trying to sneak a peek at his phone, but people were sitting all round him. He laughed silently to himself at the thought that he wished his contemporary church had old-fashioned, high-backed pews so at least no one sitting behind him could spot him taking out his phone. He felt a combination of shame for not listening intently to the sermon and frustration for not being able to access his phone without potential embarrassment. He felt trapped in temporary bondage, waiting for the service to end, when it would be acceptable even in the sanctuary to check his alerts.

New technologies offer amazing ways of connecting with people and building friendships. But unless we use them wisely, they can spread our time and energy so thin that we lack the deeper, life-giving relationships that we desperately long for. Communication technologies offer digital avenues to friendship and love. But just around the corner is a kind of technological bondage to messages from more and more people and organizations.

In this chapter we address how technologies can help and hinder interpersonal relationships. The first two sections focus on the myth of multitasking and encourage greater single-tasking in relationships. In the next two sections we suggest the importance of resisting message smothering and go on to consider the myth of perfection in relationships, especially related to the implied promises about the benefits of technological life. The last two sections focus on the importance of rest, first, and then the related significance of humor. In one sense James's discomfort is tragic; certainly he ought to be able to focus wholeheartedly on his relationship with God. But in another sense his situation, like ours, is comedic. We simply need to take our technologies and ourselves a bit less seriously and enjoy more fully the grace in our relationships with God and each other.

Embracing Single-Tasking

The jury is in. Multitasking is a myth. No one can really do it well. When we think we're multitasking, we're actually shuttling back and forth from one activity to another without closely concentrating on any one of them.[1] Multitasking is like conversing simultaneously with three people on three different phones. None of the conversations will be as good as if we conducted each one separately. Even though James was not talking with others on his phone during the worship service, the vibrating alerts were distracting him from paying attention to the sermon. He kept thinking about the possible messages on his phone rather than focusing on the message from the pulpit.

The idea of multitasking is more technological than relational. Anyone can listen to music while being active in social media. Technologically it's possible. It might even be fun. But it won't necessarily lead to better or deeper friendships.

To get to know a person well, try single-tasking in person without an agenda. Get together at a relatively quiet location, like a peaceful coffee shop or a vacant beach, without social-media interruptions.

As a next step, try setting aside fifteen minutes daily for an entire week to focus on communicating with one person without interruptions, even if it means just being together. If the person isn't available in person, on the phone, or through video on a given day, spend the time (1) reflecting on that person as a gift, recalling her or his blessings to you, and (2) praying that God will show you how to use the gift of communication to bless this person and your relationship. The last two practices are both forms of prayer that build relationships even when people are unable to be together.

As a final step toward getting to know someone well, plan longer activities that nurture leisurely, spontaneous communication. Some of the best activities include going for walks and hikes, playing games, sharing meals, and taking road trips. These kinds of activities provide excuses to meet and don't compete with conversation. They are relationally open, conversation-producing forms of multitasking. We might call them "soft" multitasking.

The goal in single-tasking is not to eliminate technology from our lives or even to avoid all multitasking. The goal is to maintain time and energy for listening and for developing relationships, especially friendships.

How we use technology in the midst of our busy lives is critically important. Technology can supplement interpersonal communication. A study by the Entertainment Software Association found that changes in both gaming technologies and the ways that people use these technologies have challenged the stereotype of the lone, male, socially awkward gamer. The average gamer is thirty-one years old, and nearly 50 percent are female. Moreover, video gamers lead more social lives and are more optimistic, more educated, emotionally closer to their families, and even more socially conscious. Finally, gamers are more likely to consider friends important in life and less likely to watch television alone.[2]

New communication technologies always have a capacity to contribute to relationships, but we have to make wise choices along the way, such as employing video games at least partly to build connections with others and avoiding the potential social isolation that games can lead to. Those who are quick to criticize gamers fail to consider that television is far more socially isolating than gaming because it is far less potentially interactive.

Understanding Multitasking

Given the relational benefits of single-tasking, why are we so prone to multitasking? First, we overly multitask because we wrongly equate mere transmission with communication. We believe the myth that faster and more efficient transmission improves communication. We even associate transmission with technology itself, as if buying the latest digital technology will necessarily improve our communication and build our relationships. We forget that *communication is shared understanding*—even shared relationship—not mere transmission. Pastoral theologian Douglas Webster says, "The substitution of momentum for meaning and a busy life for a full life robs the soul of its own music."[3]

Every new communication technology seems to promise better relationships—hence all the smiling people in smartphone advertisements. Technologies represent human progress. "Modern technologists are successors to pagan magicians," writes Eugene Peterson, author of *The Message*. "The means have changed but the spirit is the same: metal machines and psychological methods have replaced magic potions, but the intent is still to work my will on the environment, regardless. God is not in on it, or he is in on it only insofar as he can be used in ways that accommodate the lordly self."[4]

Second, we overly multitask in order to reduce our social fears.[5] Especially with new relationships, we're anxious because we don't know others well. We'd like to lessen that ambiguity, but we hesitate to get too emotionally intimate in case the relationship falls apart and we get hurt. Instead of allowing ourselves to get too obsessed with relational communication, we multitask among relational and nonrelational forms of communication. We surf the web or watch television partly so we don't have to communicate with anyone too intimately. One of the appeals of online dating and social media in general is that one can work on a number of relationships at once without having to make commitments. In the off-line world, such as on a college campus, this isn't so easy because dating is much more public and more open to the scrutiny of others.

High-tech multitasking in relationships is complicated, and thus we need to tread carefully when we try to conduct relationships online.

Unless we already know social-media friends well, it's hard to predict how they will interpret our text messages, blogs, posts, chats, and photos.

Third, we overly multitask because it can be a lot of fun. Creating more messages in more media won't necessarily improve our relationships, but it can deliver plenty of enjoyment, especially if we're comfortable with high-tech media. Just texting back and forth, responding to others' online posts, or uploading new photos can be entertaining.

But as we adopt more technologies in our lives, we can easily become extreme multitaskers. Like machines, we end up hectically trying to regulate multiple messages for maximum impact. We're continually jumping from message to message, like dodging between cars on a busy interstate highway to try to get ahead of the pack. Author and former priest Brennan Manning says, "Our controlled frenzy creates the illusion of a well-ordered existence. We move from crisis to crisis, responding to the urgent and neglecting the essential." He adds, "We still walk around. We still perform all of the gestures and actions identified as human, but we resemble people carried along on the mechanical sidewalk at an airport. The fire in the belly dies."[6]

Ironically, feelings of loneliness have increased among people who have access to plenty of communication technologies. People easily feel disconnected in the crowd of messengers.[7] Perhaps high-tech people are not getting together with others in person as often.[8] In any case, people feel lonely when their level of emotional intimacy doesn't meet expectations.[9] New communication technologies don't seem to substitute for the kind of emotional intimacy formed through in-person interaction.

Resisting Message Smothering

Rich and rewarding relationships are formed partly through listening to unpredictable dialogue. Such relationships often require working through seemingly competing and opposing desires, such as togetherness and personal independence.[10] Generous, life-affirming relationships are possible only by loosening our grip on each other and giving up some personal freedom. Smothering our friends with messages can even drive them from us. But how much is too much?

College students and parents average twenty-two calls, texts, or emails weekly. Some super-tethered parents even call to wake up their offspring on exam days. Researchers suspect that adult children aren't learning personal responsibility and that parents aren't learning to let go.[11] Moreover, some college students respond defensively to parental over-tethering by, for example, avoiding coming home, hiding personal belongings, and ignoring parents' text messages.[12] Maybe some college students are overly tethered to Mom.

Couples who text frequently might not be deeply in love. Men who text their partners frequently report lower relational quality than men who report texting their loved ones sparingly. Researchers speculate that as men disconnect from a relationship, they text in order to replace more personal, face-to-face interaction. Women, on the other hand, may text more as their relationship deteriorates in an attempt to resolve the conflict—an online version of the need "to talk things out."[13] In any case, texting is unrelated to couples' perceptions of love and commitment, whereas phone interactions are.[14] Perhaps frequent social-media use does not foster close and satisfying relationships.[15]

Even when they start online, most healthy relationships take on a multimedia life of their own as people serve each other with mutual delight, affection, and respect. In a balanced relationship, partners are comfortable talking on the phone, texting, and hanging out together. The partners don't always have to be together in person, but they value that time especially. They give each other plenty of space for relational explorations and discoveries, such as new activities that nurture mutual online or in-person delight. A high-tech and low-tech (or high-touch) balance seems to be most fitting for healthy interpersonal relationships.

Using a controlled experiment, researchers added voice communication to the existing text communication among members of an online gaming guild playing *World of Warcraft*. As a result, members of the guild tended to like and trust each other more and to avoid negative communication.[16] Apparently text messages do have relational limits.

Avoiding Perfectionism

In spite of the promises of the latest technologies, faultless communication is impossible. Our relationships are complicated. We never fully understand ourselves, let alone others. The apostle Paul admits, "For I have the desire to do what is good, but I cannot carry it out. For I do not do the good I want to do, but the evil I do not want to do—this I keep on doing."[17] We humans are not seamless messaging machines but persons who sometimes expect too much from our technologies and ourselves.

Communicative perfectionism—aiming to be flawless, machine-like communicators, and holding ourselves to such an idealistic relational standard—is unrealistic. The perfectionist "always has to have everything according to his or her design, one who fastidiously strives to never make a mistake."[18] Human perfection is a myth, maybe even an idol. No amount of study, dedication, or skill can turn anyone into an impeccable communicator. If you wait for perfect conditions, you will never get anything done, says the writer of Ecclesiastes.[19]

Perfectionism leads to critical hearts, judgmental attitudes, and destructive communication patterns. When we succumb to such an ideal, we may habitually correct others' speaking or language. We may criticize others for actions that mirror our own weaknesses; we may try to make ourselves feel better by projecting our own problems on them. For instance, a poor listener might gossip about his friend's poor listening skills, saying something like, "Boy, he doesn't get it." A verbally abusive person might disparage the same trait in friends and relatives.

In fact, perfectionistic communicators often create poor communication. "It can be absolutely agonizing to have to sit through a speech or a set of instructions from a perfectionist," write two psychologists. "It's next to impossible to glean the main points of the speech. . . . One perfectionistic salesman's internal e-mails were never read because they were too lengthy. 'We see an e-mail from Jim, and we just hit delete,' one coworker quipped."[20]

Perfectionism damages our relationships. We hold ourselves, if not others, to an unrealistic ideal. Then we can get so frustrated that we become anxious, impatient communicators. We hold grudges, struggling to forgive others and ourselves.[21] Perfectionists are impossible to please—even themselves.

Especially in romantic relationships, we tend to hold excessive expectations. For instance, we accept the myth of wedded bliss. Realistically speaking, however, no one experiences anything close to relational perfection in life—let alone in marriage. If siblings and coworkers can't entirely get along, why would spouses be able to experience relational perfection?

The notion of the perfect marriage runs deep in contemporary popular culture, from music to movies and novels. Its origins are not in Scripture but probably in romantic fiction.[22] Couples with turbulent courtships commonly assume that communication issues will evaporate once they tie the knot. Instead of addressing their issues before the wedding and working on them during the marriage, they drag old baggage into their new life together and find that communication can become even more difficult. "For whatever reason," writes Christian author Gary Chapman, "one failure after another is ignored until a long, high, thick wall develops between two people who started out 'in love.' Communication grinds to a halt and only resentment remains."[23]

In relationships, perfectionism sets us up for repeated disappointments. In seeking to be loved by others for being perfect, we become less and less lovable, failing to meet even our own expectations and rejecting others' attempts to initiate an intimate relationship with us. We lack mercy on ourselves. We get frustrated and perhaps even angry with others and ourselves. Some emotional difficulties, including compulsive eating disorders, apparently result from wearisome perfectionism.[24]

Communicative realism—an honest sense of everyone's limited communicative abilities and related communicative imperfections—is a lot healthier emotionally and spiritually than idealistic perfectionism. As Christian realists, we work hard but not obsessively, recognizing that striving to do our best is not the same as perfectionism.[25] We accept responsibility for our communication and the resulting relationships. We know that God wants us to flourish, but we also know that we're flawed communicators. So we learn to live within our human limits. Author Wendell Berry writes, "We must address ourselves seriously, and not a little fearfully, to the problem of human scale. What is it? How do we stay within it? The reason is simply that we cannot live except within limits, and these limits are of many kinds: spatial, material, moral, and spiritual."[26]

Our goal should be to develop our communicative skills realistically in the context of the Spirit's guidance, God's grace, and an understanding community. We invite God's ongoing communion with us as we muddle through everyday relationships. We can call humbly on a combination of skill and faith. Rather than relying merely on our own technological expertise, we can share in both the responsibilities and joys of developing our relationships with God and others. We can let go of our excessive standards for others and ourselves. After all, says Scot McKnight in *The Jesus Creed: Loving God, Loving Others*, the "goal of a disciple of Jesus is relationship, not perfection."[27]

Faith in God is a critically important antidote for communicative perfectionism. It helps us in at least three ways.

Faith keeps us from suffering the weight of thinking that we will be judged and found lacking for all of our communicative failures.

Jesus's death and resurrection cover the gap between our flawless and faulty communication. We don't need to obsess about communication because Jesus will forgive us for our failures. Of course, we shouldn't take Jesus's grace for granted. But neither should we discount the eternal value of Jesus's love for us. Jesus is Lord of grace, not legalism. He is transforming our hearts and renewing our minds, not holding us to unreachable expectations.

Faith reminds us of our ever-present companion in everyday communication: the Holy Spirit.

Unless we daily acknowledge the presence of the Holy Spirit in our communication, we can depend too much on our own communicative abilities and not enough on the presence of God. Some people constantly analyze and reanalyze scenarios: What if I said x instead of z? What if I sent an email instead of called? What should I wear to impress my new acquaintance? While these questions are worth asking, they are merely human questions. A deeper one is, "What is the Spirit already doing in my relationships, and how can I communicate in tune with the existing work of the Spirit?"

The Spirit is ready to serve us. For instance, using only one word, define for yourself the type of communication that you need from a specific person (e.g., forgiveness, appreciation, encouragement, joy, and respect—and don't let this short list limit your reflections). Then ask the Spirit to alert you to an opportunity to humbly express your need to this person. Be vigilant but patient, considering when the other person might be least defensive and most receptive. Then explain what you need, not what's wrong with the other person. Finally, if the time seems right, ask your friend to express one of her or his one-word needs to you.

Faith focuses not just on our strengths but also on our weaknesses.

God is sometimes manifest in our shortcomings rather than our apparent strengths. By all accounts Moses was a poor speaker, perhaps the last person one would expect God to nominate to address Pharaoh and the Israelites. The apostle Paul boasted about the things that demonstrated his human weaknesses to the churches he served. In 2 Corinthians, he exposes his weaknesses and troubles to other believers, identifying them as "participants with him in the life of the church."[28] God, through the work of the Spirit, is able and willing to make his glory manifest in our inelegant or inarticulate communication.

In other words, the Spirit is our special guide in understanding how to communicate in specific situations. Communication principles and skills can help us, but they are only part of the story. When we walk by faith, we have a more mature sense of how best to serve others with the gift of communication, even if we aren't highly accomplished communicators. We're more apt to take the right risks, such as being vulnerable and transparent in appropriate settings. We're more likely to speak up or remain silent at the right time—what is called *kairos* in Greek, God's perfect timing, pregnant with opportunity for shared understanding.[29]

Communicating in the Spirit, we are especially less likely to be impetuous, such as by texting or speaking instantly without first listening. We will more patiently use language in ways that reflect the fruit of the Spirit in our lives—love, joy, peace, patience, kindness, goodness, faithfulness, gentleness, and self-control.[30] As a result, we will love others better and will be more lovable. You might try displaying, in a place where you will regularly see it during the day, a note that simply states one fruit of the Spirit. Each time you see it, remind yourself that the Spirit is with you and that you should humbly walk with the Spirit by embodying that fruit in your communication. From a Christian perspective this builds virtue by helping us focus on the quality of our character rather than the quantity of our messaging.

Resting in Grace

We can labor so hard and long in life that we sour our relationships. The singer Michael Jackson once proclaimed, "I'm a perfectionist; I'll work until I drop."[31] Sadly, he did. And his interpersonal relationships were tragic.

When our communication is no longer fun it becomes a burdensome chore. It stresses us out. Life becomes work without play, labor without delight. Listening and speaking become hassles rather than joys. The German theologian Dietrich Bonhoeffer warns, "For us the creatureliness and miraculousness of the day has completely disappeared. We have deprived the day of its power. We no longer allow ourselves to be determined by the day. We count and compute it, we do not allow the day to give to us."[32]

We're not created solely to work at communication or anything else. According to the book of Genesis, God rested on the seventh day, after creating the world. He looked at the fruit of his labor and enjoyed it. God himself relaxed. God, who in Scripture spoke the world into existence, ceased speaking in order to delight in his work.

That's the creational pattern for us too. We labor, but we also break. We work at developing relationships, but we also spend time enjoying relationships. We speak, but we also listen, especially to all of the signs of grace in our lives. Seminary professor Bruce Birch writes,

"To take seriously what it means to be called into relationship with a radically free God means that some of our energies ought always to be devoted to scanning the horizon looking for the grace-bringing, wholesome-making activity of God and joining it, rather than thinking, once we get things organized, God will be obligated to join us."[33]

From a biblical perspective, interpersonal communication is meant to be pleasure as well as effort. If we don't relish some communication, our relationships will become more of a painstaking curse than a special blessing. Our communicative effort and delight are meant to be complementary; each builds up the other. We need to be able to simply enjoy relating to people—to "rest" in relationships as well as labor at them.

Couples say that their relationships are much more fulfilling when they have fun together. Happy couples laugh together.[34] For them, enjoyment isn't just an indulgence. It's essential for the life of their relationships. One researcher even developed a fun-and-friendship survey to measure couples' pleasure in spending time together, asking couples to indicate the extent to which they agreed with statements like, "We regularly have great conversations where we just talk as good friends" and "My partner really listens to me when I have something important to say."[35] Flourishing together relationally requires fun and friendship.

In the ancient Hebrew and Christian traditions, much of life's delight comes through festive rest. Believers rest not just to cease work but also to celebrate all of their blessings. This is why Sunday, the Lord's Day, is also traditionally the day for rest (Sabbath) and worship. We gather on the first day of the week to give thanks to God for his mercy and grace. We celebrate all blessings, especially God's gift of salvation. We thank God for his work in the world and in our lives. Historically many Jews celebrated by making love on the Sabbath as well.

In worship, we remind ourselves that we can't save ourselves—and that God has already saved us through Jesus Christ. We let go of all our pretensions, all our efforts to self-create heaven in our relationships. We accept God's blessings, respond in gratitude, and prepare to return to work on Monday. Rest and worship together begin each week; after worship, we "go in peace to love and serve the Lord"—a phrase used at the conclusion of many Roman Catholic and Protestant services as a charge to the congregation.

One of the great ironies of becoming more faithful communicators is that we have to give up some of the very control that we want to exercise. We have to repeatedly offer ourselves to God as living sacrifices, dead to our own wills and alive to Christ. We have to pay attention to what the Spirit is already doing in our relationships rather than focus just on what we want out of our relationships. The more

---

THE SERENITY PRAYER

God grant me the serenity to accept the things I cannot change;
the courage to change the things I can;
and the wisdom to know the difference.

Reinhold Neibuhr

---

bloated we are with our own agendas, the less room there is in our hearts and minds for the often-surprising work of the Spirit.

Resting from and giving thanks for our communication revives our souls. Keeping a Sabbath in our lives frees us to experience afresh the delight and wonder of everyday existence. Without rest, we lose our sense of childlike joy. We become messaging machines trying to dictate our futures. Rest helps us to "get the adult maturity to keep our feet on the ground and retain the childlike innocence to make the leap of faith."[36]

Laughing at Ourselves

In the ancient story of the Tower of Babel, the mighty Babylonians built a great tower into the heavens to make a name for themselves. Using human-made bricks, they cleverly constructed a kind of stairway to heaven.

Then God "came down" to see what they were doing. Clearly they didn't quite climb all the way up to the heavenly realms to shake hands with their Creator. Once God sized up their arrogance, he confused their language so they couldn't continue working together on their monument to themselves. In effect, God apparently protected the Babylonians from their own arrogance by mixing up their communication.

The story is probably meant to be humorous. The Babylonians were conceited fools who thought they could play God. Arrogantly aiming to make a name for themselves, they ended up unable to use language—represented as the gift of "naming"—to collaborate on their folly. God humbled them; he brought them back down to earth, to the humus. Previously they could collaborate fully on their arrogant plans; after God created linguistic confusion, the Babylonians couldn't even understand each other. They aimed to connect directly with God but ended up jabbering, unable to connect with each other.

We all live with a kind of Babylonian strain in our communication-related DNA. We sometimes think too highly of our abilities, and we reach out to befriend and work with those who share our arrogance about building relationships, organizations, and institutions that will impress others. Then something happens and we're humbly brought back down to earth. It might be a terrible misunderstanding that we were clueless about and that leads to a falling out among leaders. It might be the sudden arrival of a "Dear John" or "Dear Sally" note indicating that we no longer have a romantic friend, or an unexpectedly bad job-performance review. A wake-up call arrives, and we're forced to reconsider how well we really communicate. Our name is tarnished—even to ourselves.

Should we get angry? Sad? How should we respond to such signs of weakness? If we were treated fairly and simply failed, we need to regroup. We've been dealt some humility, probably merited. The apostle Paul said that he would boast about the things that showed his weakness because God's grace was sufficient.[37]

But if we were control freaks bent on using the gift of communication to make a name for ourselves, we've got some explaining to do. We've been cut down to size. We can see ourselves once again for who we are—namely, God's creatures rather than God himself. We can laugh at ourselves—at our pretense. What were we thinking? Why did we rely so much on our own abilities and so little on God's wisdom and grace? We can look in the mirror and see a circus clown who has fumbled and fallen. As renowned priest and author Henri Nouwen puts it, "The clowns remind us with a tear and a smile that we share the same human weakness."[38]

One of the best signs of a healthy relationship is the ability to laugh together at ourselves. If we take each other too seriously, we won't enjoy each other as much. We need to be able to tell humorous stories about our own weaknesses and foibles. Humor not only cuts us down to human size; it also builds us up in mutual grace.

Humor can help emotionally hurting people. "Personal transgressions" are "nontraumatic social interactions that victims nonetheless perceive to be morally wrong and personally hurtful."[39] In other words, someone feels personally wronged and experiences emotional hurt as a result. People with a greater sense of humor seem to cope with and even overcome such transgressions.[40] Moreover, a person's sense of humor might benefit relationship partners as well.[41] Humor helps us to not take ourselves too seriously and to give others more space for actions that could otherwise seem like personal transgressions.

"Comedy," writes spiritual theologian James Houston, "is a good instrument whereby we see the false idols of our world, and knock them down. As finite beings, with infinite desires, we live comical lives, full of incongruities."[42] In laughter we rediscover the freedom from excessive busyness, technological overkill, and personal pretense. We take off masks and live in unity with the Holy Spirit, who reveals the faithful route to flourishing.

Conclusion

High-tech society provides many amazing communication technologies that connect us with family, church, work, politics, news, entertainment, and even dates. Our lives are tapestries of mediated relationships, online and in person.

We have to remind ourselves to let go of our busyness—especially our multitasking—in order to regain a proper sense of who and whose we are. No matter how hard we work at communicating, perfection is impossible. Relationships are far too complicated and dynamic.

Moreover, excessive work robs us of the sheer pleasure of relationships. So we periodically rest, like God. And we worship the one true God who is indeed in charge of the universe. We give up our pretense and climb back down to earth with the clowns. We let go, knowing that God will catch us.

Regular worship, restful times, good friends, and a healthy sense of humor will quiet our excessive alerts. James could have laughed at himself for wanting to use his cell phone secretly during worship. What was he thinking? What messages on his phone would have been more important than the sermon? James could have shared his folly with some friends so they could laugh together. Why didn't he just turn off his phone?

The next chapter considers how our communication forms and deforms our identities. Both the ways we think about ourselves and how we view others are shaped by the ways we communicate and miscommunicate. When we order our desires properly—to love God, neighbor, and self—we are more prone to use the gift of communication to serve others and glorify God.

4

....

KNOW YOURSELF

The TV series *The Office* expressed it well: coworkers can be jerks. Not just funny jerks. Nasty ones. *The Wall Street Journal* agreed in its 2009 feature "The Fall of the Workplace Jerk."[1]

Variations on office jerks include *passive-aggressive communicators* who wait until they're boiling mad before complaining about anything—and then blast away at others; *gossipers* who are everyone's acquaintances and no one's true friend; and *obnoxious* colleagues who talk too loudly on the phone, invade others' office spaces, wear inappropriate clothing—too formal, too informal, too revealing, too showy—and order highly aromatic food to eat in the office, only to smirk about their resulting gastrointestinal distress.

As the hit sitcom *The Office* often demonstrates, each of us has two identities. One is our *self-identity*—how we see ourselves or what we think we're like as persons. Each of the characters in *The Office* saw himself or herself as a particular kind of person. Few, if any, saw themselves as office jerks.

Our *social identity* is how others see us. The ancient Greek rhetoricians used the term *ethos* to capture a person's image or character as perceived by others. Some of the humor in *The Office* is based on the difference between how characters perceive themselves and how their colleagues see them—the difference between their self-identities and their social identities.

In interpersonal communication, others might perceive us differently than we perceive ourselves. To put it differently, our self-identities can deceive us. For instance, we might be overlooking a bit of jerk inside each of us. Given our nature, we're not just inept communicators. We're wrongful, even self-serving communicators. We don't always use the gift of communication to love others as we should. We're too self-focused—all of us, without exception.[2] To use the biblical metaphor, we have logs in our eyes.[3]

In this chapter we explore how our self-identities are formed and how we can better conform both our self-identities and our social identities to the biblical standard of persons who love God, neighbor, and self. First, we address two identity-forming tendencies in human nature: avoiding communication (cocooning) and criticizing others.[4] Next, we explore the role of human desire in interpersonal communication. Typically our desires shape how and why we communicate. Finally, we advocate for a responsible approach to interpersonal communication as *social action* (not just *personal expression*) for which we all will be held accountable. By watching over our identities we can better seek to be more faithful and virtuous as well as skilled communicators.

Cocooning

One identity-forming pattern in human communication is *cocooning*—willfully avoiding people either because we fear having to relate to them or because we want to make them feel bad. Cocooning takes many forms, but a helpful model is Adam and Eve after their fall from grace. At the serpent's urging, they ate from the fruit of the tree of life. As Scripture puts it, they both disobeyed God's only cautionary command, felt ashamed, and subsequently tried to hide from God and each other. Apparently filled with shame, they lost their innocence and clothed themselves. Their solution was to cocoon themselves away from their Creator and each other.

A common form of cocooning is the *silent treatment* (sometimes called *stonewalling*), when we stop talking to someone to retaliate for something she or he supposedly did to us. We pretend like that person doesn't exist. We offer her no respect. We talk with ourselves negatively about the person we're stonewalling; we chat up a storm in our own mind about how she wronged us. Maybe we even ignore the person on social media, giving her a sort of digital cold shoulder.

The silent treatment is like bullying—a way of ostracizing others. Often the silent person uses the withdrawal of direct, verbal communication to try to get what he or she wants, such as power, recognition, or superiority. Confronting such silent bullies often doesn't work; instead it leads to verbal conflict.

Another approach is to continue to love the silent person with your own actions and words. This should be genuine, humble love—not forced love to try to make the bully feel wrong. It's up to the bully to reach out to you; it's not up to you to repair the relationship on the bully's terms.

In the case of Adam and Eve, their previous desire for communion with God and each other was apparently overshadowed by their desire to protect their fragile self-identities. Facing God was embarrassing. Facing each other was awkward. The two dealt with their situation by cocooning. It was like they just wanted to stay in bed after sunrise, hiding under the blanket with a pillow over their heads, the phone turned off, and the bedroom door closed.

One way to interpret this biblical account is that human nature is so corrupted that we can't possibly live in perfectly open, completely honest, guilt-free relationships. Our consciences tell us that we've treated others wrongly. We live with interpersonal wounds that need constant care. We cocoon both to protect ourselves from hurt and to hurt others. But in the process we stop communicating about important things, including broken relationships and injustices right before our eyes.

Transparency—openly, honestly, and appropriately sharing what's on our minds and in our hearts—is the opposite of cocooning. When we live transparently in trusting relationships, we learn much about each other, including some of the deepest desires of our hearts. We can love and serve each other more fully because we accept each other in spite of our weaknesses. Our listening becomes shared, aimed at mutual flourishing, and grounded in genuine social identities.

Criticizing

The second identity-forming tendency in our communication is putting people down. After Adam and Eve disobeyed their Creator, God confronted them. Adam blamed Eve, who first ate the forbidden fruit and passed it along to Adam. Then Eve blamed the serpent. They both criticized others for their own, willful misdeeds. It was a "he-made-me-do-it" or "she-made-me-do-it" scenario.

Criticizing—blaming others for something that we perceive as unacceptable, often to make ourselves feel superior—is a common problem with our communication. There are times when we should confront others about the ways they have wronged us (e.g., to seek an apology[5]), but much of our criticism is wrongly designed to make us feel better about ourselves by belittling others.

We all know that we're imperfect. We see firsthand our communicative failures, such as the ways we ignore and hurt others, fail to advocate for those in need, and advance self-serving agendas. When it comes to loving our neighbors as ourselves, we repeatedly miss the mark. We sometimes compensate by trying to build ourselves up through speaking negatively of others—often criticizing others for the very kinds of relationship-sinking communication that we ourselves practice. In short, we selectively look outside ourselves for the causes of our own misdeeds. We care more about saving face than being honest.

Addressing our self-identities partly means not blaming others for our weaknesses. "You made me do it" is one of the greatest lies of all time. Whenever we say it, we falsely tell ourselves that we didn't have a choice to respond the way we did. We play the victim. We justify our inappropriate communication based on our own feelings. We transfer responsibility to someone else. We always need to ask ourselves if the facts support such a one-sided self-defense.

When we dig deeper into our guilt and embarrassment, we uncover something even more disturbing. We can become jealous when others are more faithful, skillful, or accomplished than we are. We can even harbor ill will in our hearts toward those who are better communicators and perhaps more popular or successful. Truth be told, we sometimes like it when popular people fail. Occasionally we justify our animosity by telling ourselves that admired people are self-righteous and deserve to be taken down a few notches when they experience public embarrassment that tarnishes their social identities.

When negative conflict brews, we're quick to indict others yet slow to admit our part in the mess. When things go wrong, we prefer to blame others.[6] Physically abusive spouses blame their partners for their destructive behaviors.[7] Workers blame bosses. Students blame teachers. Friends blame friends. This is human nature.

The main difficulty we face in assessing our critical attitudes toward others is that criticism is not altogether bad. There are aspects of our relationships that are simply wrong. Like all sins, they are "not the way it's supposed to be."[8] Yet our criticisms of others often point to what's wrong with us. In fact, we're hypervigilant with others' problems that mirror ours.

Checking Our Desires

To discern if we're practicing destructive cocooning and criticism, we need to check and recheck our motives. What do we desire when we withhold communication from others or when we disparage them? What do we really want? Recognition? Respect? Love? Understanding? Our communication reflects our desires, especially what we seek *from* others and *for* ourselves.

The wise writer of Proverbs says that just as water reflects a face, so one's life reflects the heart's desires.[9] We have the abilities to learn communication skills, master communication theories, and memorize communication-related definitions. But what do we truly long for? *Why* do we communicate?

Corrupted desires lead us astray. We all know people who love to speak just to impress people. They don't listen. They seem to be overly enamored with their own rhetorical abilities. Life is all about them. Maybe we are that way too.

Before responding to someone who is short or impatient with you, try asking yourself three questions about your motives: (1) Are you trying to get even or to heal the relationship? (2) Are you trying to put down or build up the other person? (3) What do you desire from the other person and for yourself?

Many office jerks are adept communicators; they know how to get a message across. But their desires are warped. They care more about their own agendas, successes, fun, and fears than about others' flourishing.

Communication competence is the ability to communicate appropriately and effectively in particular situations. It includes knowledge, skill, and motivation. We're more competent communicators when we know what to communicate (knowledge) and how to communicate (skill) in particular contexts and when we seek to communicate well (motivation).[10] But even such competent communication is not always sufficient. The way the term is typically used, "competence" doesn't include virtue or character—that is, the kind of person one is as reflected in what she or he truly desires. For instance, one can be a competent but self-serving and even manipulative speaker.

In short, faithful and virtuous communication flows from a desire to love God and neighbor. Communicative skill without righteous desire can dangerously lead us to exploit others. Relationships dissolve over this lack of humble self-awareness. Does our communication tend to invite others to lean on our shoulders for encouragement and support, or does it find fault in them?

Ordering Our Desires

The secret to linking healthy desires to our communication is understanding and then ordering our desires properly.[11] It's the threefold law of love: to love God, neighbor, and self. Used in that order to guide our communication, these love-based desires lead us to recognize our misguided practices, seek the best for others, and pursue personal flourishing along the way. Such proper ordering of desires helps unify our self-identities and social identities.

Here's how our desires should work together in our communication.

Desire #1—Loving God

We gratefully desire to communicate under God's authority, according to God's wishes, to bring honor and glory to God.

Desire #2—Loving Our Neighbors

We desire to communicate on behalf of other people, who are our "neighbors" made in God's own image and likeness. We are called to serve and advocate for them just as the Holy Spirit advocates for us to the Father. We offer the fruit of our communication skills to advance the interests of others. Under God's grace, we become living sacrifices, using our talents and skills to demonstrate Jesus's love to others in all areas of life.

Of course this kind of neighborly communication is not always easy to discern. It takes diligence and experience. Suppose you appear to be the sole witness to an auto accident except for the two parties involved in the crash. You know who caused the accident. Should you continue on your way? Stop and console the victims? Call the police? Wait for the police to arrive so you can offer an objective report of what happened? Assuming no one was badly injured, who is your neighbor in this case? What should you desire? How should you use your gift of communication?

Desire #3—Loving Ourselves

Finally, we desire to communicate on behalf of ourselves. We take into account our own needs and interests—what's good and right for each of us as followers of Jesus. We don't give away all of our communicative time and effort to the point of destroying our own life, including our relationships with others. We advocate for ourselves, humbly as well as skillfully, just as we advocate for our neighbors.

In other words, we love ourselves as neighbors too. This might sound selfish. Yet the gift of communication equips us to communicate with ourselves (sometimes called *intrapersonal communication*[12]) just as we communicate with God and other neighbors.

To put it differently, desires 2 and 3—love of neighbor and self—are equally important even though we are called in most circumstances to put our neighbors' interests ahead of our own. In fact, to acquire

---

LISTEN TO YOURSELF FOR YOURSELF

In order to love ourselves as communicators, we need to ask ourselves tough questions.

- How well am I caring for myself with the gift of communication?
- Am I so focused on communicating with others that I don't even know what I think or how I should think?
- Have I been attending to my own communication skills?
- Am I listening to my own heart?
- Am I so busy that I neglect to take care of myself?

The great preacher Charles Spurgeon wrote, "It would be in vain for me to stock my libraries . . . if I neglect the culture of myself; . . . my own spirit, soul, and body are my nearest machinery for sacred service; my spiritual faculties, and my inner life, are my battle-ax and weapons of war."

Quote from Charles H. Spurgeon, *Lectures to My Students* (Peabody, MA: Hendrickson, 2010), 8–9.

---

the skill to serve our neighbors, we must also attend to our own relational health. This self-neighbor connection is complicated and untidy. We have to be on guard against justifying selfishness, such as getting in someone's good graces by promising to pray for them when we know that we won't or rationalizing deceptive résumé language

THE FOUR MOST MARRIAGE-DESTROYING HABITS

1. Criticism—stating one's complaints as a defect in one's partner's personality (i.e., giving the partner negative trait attributions). Example: "You always talk about yourself. You're so selfish."
2. Contempt—statements that come from a relative position of superiority. Contempt is the greatest predictor of divorce and must be eliminated. Example: "You're an idiot."
3. Defensiveness—self-protection in the form of righteous indignation or innocent victimhood. Defensiveness wards off a perceived attack. Example: "It's not my fault that we're always late; it's your fault."
4. Stonewalling—emotional withdrawal from interaction. Example: The listener does not give the speaker the usual nonverbal signals that the listener is "tracking" the speaker.

Psychologist John Gottman calls these destructive communicative practices "The Four Horsemen of the Apocalypse."

Adapted from John M. Gottman and Nan Silver, *The Seven Principles for Making Marriage Work: A Practical Guide from the Country's Foremost Relationship Expert* (New York: Three Rivers, 2000), 27–34. This summary is from "Research FAQs," The Gottman Institute, http://www.gottman.com/research/research-faqs/.

in order to advance our careers—a practice that will also tarnish our self-identities. But we also have to guard against being so completely selfless that we destroy our capacity to use the gift of communication to love God and neighbor.

In order to keep a healthy, God-focused balance, we need to be anchored in a Christian community where worship, fellowship, and education form us into healthy lovers of God, neighbor, and self—all at the same time, and in the right order. Faithful communities nurture life-giving interpersonal communication. They help us to act rightly by syncing our self-identities and social identities with the righteous desires and good practices of a faith community.

Communicating Responsibly

Communicating with right desires comes from the heart, but the result of such communication is evident in our actions. In fact, human communication is *action* (proactive doing) rather than mere *behavior* (passively responding to stimuli).[13] Our communication isn't a simple stimulus-response mechanism caused by our social environment. No one causes us to say, write, or paint something in particular simply because of what they say, write, or show to us. No one causes us to dress or speak offensively, to gossip, or to stonewall. No one causes us to speak unkindly or to listen impatiently. Bad role models can lead us astray, but we still chart our own ways. Communication is action that is based on our decisions and flows from our desires. It's meant to be a way of responsibly practicing the three loves by making right choices.

A simplistic behavioral model of human communication doesn't capture how God made us as inventive, active communicators called to responsibly love God, neighbor, and self. Human communication is amazingly creative and deeply relational. There are over one million words in English alone, addressing hundreds of thousands of life-related topics. When we put our self-identities and our social identities on watch, we admit that we're responsible creatures who act intentionally upon our desires.

So, at root, interpersonal communication isn't just about processing messages. It's about living responsibly in relationships. This is why the word "communication" can be so deceptive. The word is so general and so non–human specific that it doesn't capture the life-forming and life-destroying nature of human communication within relationships. We don't just communicate; we don't just behave. We perform incredibly important and highly moral actions, such as inviting, accepting, promising, forgiving, and committing. Our communicative actions have consequences. High school student Phoebe Prince killed herself after having been "teased incessantly, taunted by text messages and harassed on social networking sites."[14] Words exercise power.

Also, responsible human communication isn't just about self-expression. If we used the gift of communication only to express ourselves, there wouldn't be much shared understanding. Our communication would be dismally self-serving—designed merely to advance our ego. We'd just be talking past each other. Communication is more about collectively seeking mutual understanding than individually performing self-expression. As leadership expert John Maxwell puts it, "Good communication and leadership are all about connecting."[15]

The fact that we're called to be responsible communicators is clear in the extent to which we are intentional about it. We often think about what we're going to say or not say.[16] We plan important conversations and presentations, from wedding vows to apologies. We revise them. We rehearse some of them in our minds—like proposing marriage, sharing our faith, or prepping for a job interview. We worry about which words and gestures to use and how to express them. If we aren't adequately intentional, we know we might speak regrettably. We might come across as being unprepared, incompetent, or even offensive—all three of which suggest irresponsibility.

When our hearts are rightly engaged, we approach all communicative actions responsibly, watching out for God's will and our neighbor's interests. We can't always be prepared for what will happen in conversations, but we can listen carefully and avoid being intentionally self-serving.

Moving Forward Faithfully

For Christians, communicative action is meant to be faithful. We acknowledge our broken and fragmented selves, and move forward, knowing that God has given us power to overcome our hurts and insecurities. We continually remind ourselves that we are created in God's image. We are his children. His beloved. And his love is not based on what we have done or failed to do. God loves us unconditionally. We don't have to criticize to feel worthy. Brennan Manning writes, "Self-acceptance becomes possible only through radical trust in Jesus' acceptance of me as I am."[17]

We are not created to defeat ourselves with words of insecurity and inferiority. This is tough for many of us who struggle with a sense of low self-worth, convincing ourselves that we will never be good enough. We aren't rich enough. Attractive enough. Smart enough. Athletic enough. Such self-deflating talk about ourselves wreaks havoc on relationships. As Manning puts it, how can we possibly "accept love from another human being when we do not love ourselves, much less accept that God could possibly love us?"[18]

So instead of hiding, we responsibly take risks. We transparently let other people enter into our lives by sharing our lives with them. We talk with special others about matters of the soul. We express our hurts and share our dreams. It requires trust. It takes courage. But we do it, knowing that God can bless our relationships.

Such self-disclosure can be honest and helpful online as well as in person. In-person support groups like Weight Watchers have long been effective ways for people with shared concerns to be transparent with each other. Women with breast cancer who disclose their stressful experiences in online support groups tend to have "greater improvements in health self-efficacy, emotional well-being, and functional well-being, and fewer breast cancer concerns."[19]

We confidently do what we must. It may be that we are asked to befriend a lonely person or seek forgiveness from one we have harmed. It may not be easy, but we can't just sit or mope around, hoping for better relationships. We need to act in tune with the guidance of the Holy Spirit.

We live in a fallen world where undeniably bad things are said (sins of *commission*) and good things are left unsaid (sins of *omission*). We really have no idea whether a friend will break our confidence or say something that hurts us deeply. We can choose, however, to have faith in the relationship. We can choose to believe the best of our friend and to believe in the unfolding beauty of the relationship. All such faith in others makes sense because of our faith in God. "Imagination is the capacity to see people in light of the hope of the wholeness that God intends for them," says philosopher Caroline Simon.[20]

Conclusion

So we approach our communication by regularly keeping watch over our self- and social identities. We don't assume that only other people are office jerks. We honestly ask ourselves if we are on the right track, growing not just in our communicative skills but also in virtue and faithfulness. Our goal is self-honesty and improvement, not perfection. The three loves—of God, neighbor, and self—provide both the proper desires and the right order for the decisions we make about how to act in communication situations.

A show like *The Office* bases much of its comedy on the gap between employees' awkward or foolish social actions and their clueless sense of self-identity. The characters do embody some stereotypes but nonetheless point to real issues in our own communication.

In the next chapter we address the importance of faithfulness in relationships, especially honesty, transparency, and authenticity. Honesty includes both being true (faithful) to one another and being truthful (speaking the truth). It also means avoiding gossip and flattery. In order to flourish in relationships, we need to be forthright persons who represent ourselves honestly as well as skillfully.

5

....
....

RELATE OPENLY

Sharon and her college-freshman daughter texted back and forth one October day. Sharon gladly received her daughter's upbeat messages peppered with smiley faces and heart emoticons. Her daughter seemed to be doing so well at college.

Actually, Sharon's daughter had been crying and showing signs of depression. Later that night she even attempted suicide. Sharon was stunned to discover her daughter's deep distress.

Sharon's daughter used social media to paint a rosy picture of how she was adapting to college life.[1] Probably to keep her mother from worrying—but also perhaps to avoid feeling shame—she misled her mother.

Like Sharon's troubled daughter, we all sometimes fail to communicate honestly and openly. Sadly, many troubled persons hide their underlying fears, doubts, and even self-destructive desires. In order to achieve deeper, richer, more relational interpersonal communication, we have to work at being both transparent and honest.

On the one hand, the daughter should have been more open with her mother. On the other hand, perhaps the mother had created a relational climate that made it difficult for her daughter to confide in her. Both she and her daughter owed it to each other to be as truthful and transparent as possible even while protecting some personal privacy.

In this chapter we explain that faithful interpersonal communication involves mutual obligations to be true (faithful) to one another. Such faithfulness includes *honesty* (avoiding intentionally false statements) and *transparency* (revealing how we feel inside). The combination of honesty and transparency is *authenticity*, which results in interpersonal communicators, especially friends and family, who know one another. Finally, we discuss the importance of telling the truth, which nurtures trust in relationships.

Being True Communicators

Relationships involve mutual obligations—what we owe each other when we seek to be true to each other. One way to understand such obligations is to say that we should be faithful to one another. What did Sharon and her daughter owe each other in order for them to be faithful as mother and daughter? What do parents and adult children owe each other? What about close friends?

Faithfulness is critically important for every relationship. What do an employer and employee, for example, owe each other if they seek to be faithful? Specifically, what does a boss owe an employee who is being terminated? Does the employee have a right to a personal termination meeting—or is it acceptable to terminate someone via email? What does a student who cheated on an exam owe the teacher when the two of them meet to discuss the exam? How can a teacher and student be true to each other?

Often these communicative obligations are difficult to discern. They can be subjective, ethical issues that require moral reasoning about right and wrong. There are at least two things to remember about being true by communicating faithfully.

We communicate in the context of God's ongoing love,
especially the promptings of the Holy Spirit.

We depend on God to equip us, inspire us, and direct our communication. We're not autonomous communicators. Even when our human relationships look grim, God can actively renew them by prompting us to listen humbly, nurturing gratitude in our hearts, and ultimately giving us the right words to say at the right times. The Spirit is always present in our interpersonal communication because he is present with us. We owe it to God to acknowledge daily his ongoing investment in our relationships. God loves us enough to be intimately present in our communication. Perhaps our consciences are a key way that the Spirit prompts us.

As soon as we slip into a kind of autonomous sense that we are completely in control of our communication, we are prone to become unfaithful, self-seeking communicators merely chasing our own desires. Often we fail to be faithful communicators because we wrongly assume that the Holy Spirit is absent. We forget God's enduring love for us, and we depend only on our own abilities. We communicate with others as if God is not personally involved in our relationships.

Research shows an important correlation between how we communicate with God and how frequently and honestly we communicate with each other. Open, authentic communicators tend to be more spiritual—and vice versa.[2] For instance, parents' frequent and honest communication more positively impacts their adolescents' spirituality than does any other parenting style. Parents' attitudes toward their children, as evident in the parents' communication, nurtures or suffocates their children's communion with God.

God loves us partly by sending the Spirit to guide us; we love God, in return, by prayerfully seeking the promptings of the Spirit. Prayer is critically important for discerning how the Spirit is guiding our communication. In prayer we suppress our own egos and humbly seek the guidance of the Spirit. The question for us every day is not just "What would Jesus do?" but also "What is the Spirit already doing?" "What relationships is God opening up in my life?" "Who among my friends needs special encouragement today?" "Am I truly listening to my colleague or just thinking about what I need to accomplish?"

Regular prayer—an ongoing, intimate relationship with God—helps us to remain mindful of the work of the Spirit throughout the day and to be true to our calling to follow Jesus Christ.

We communicate according to God's will,
especially his biblical commands.

Scripture is loaded with advice about how we should communicate if we aim to be responsibly true and transparent to God and neighbor. In fact, communication is one of the main topics in Proverbs. We owe it to God to learn and practice biblical communication.

The book of James, which emphasizes the importance of good works as evidence of faith, directly addresses how we should communicate. James compares our tongue to the rudder of a ship; our speech directs our lives, leading us on or off course.[3]

Being a faithful communicator is a dynamic calling to live obediently in relationship with God and neighbor. We need to know both how the Spirit is directing us and how God expects us to interact with others. Clearly this is much more than being a skilled communicator. We have to learn when, how, and why to use our skills in ways that will please God and demonstrate our love of neighbor and self.

COMMUNICATIVE WISDOM FROM THE BOOK OF JAMES

- "Everyone should be quick to listen, slow to speak and slow to become angry" (1:19).
- "The tongue is a small part of the body, but it makes great boasts" (3:5).
- "With the tongue we praise our Lord and Father, and with it we curse human beings, who have been made in God's likeness" (3:9).
- "Brothers and sisters, do not slander one another" (4:11).
- "Do not swear—not by heaven or by earth or by anything else. All you need to say is a simple 'Yes' or 'No'" (5:12).

God calls us, especially through the teachings of Jesus Christ, to look to him for wisdom and discernment. Our vertical relationship with God forms our horizontal relationships with other persons. As spiritual theologian Eugene Peterson writes, we live "not by what we know, but by trusting in the God who is for us. We live not by moral projects but by obedient faith."[4] We owe it to God, neighbor, and self to faithfully communicate in tune with God's Word.

Portraying Our True Self

Thanks to social media and digital editing software, it's easier than ever to portray ourselves online in a flattering light. Every text, image, and sound is a chance to create a more positive representation of who we are. The daughter in the opening story of this chapter relied on these media to create a false sense that she was thriving in college.

One problem with self-showcasing, however, is that we can become pretty good at projecting a false self, a mask we wear partly to protect our inner, vulnerable self.[5] In other words, the social self that we project is not always our true self—it's inauthentic. When we're *authentic* (transparent and honest), we say what we mean and mean what we say. When we're *inauthentic*, we concoct a false social identity to hide our real self.

Also, self-showcasing creates a kind of competitive online environment in which people feel they don't meet others' standards. One-third of Facebook users report being unhappy after visiting the social networking site. Why? Facebook envy—comparing our own real life "with our 'friends'' glossy representations of themselves"—triggers a deep sense of inadequacy and discontentment. The more time we spend on Facebook, the more we think others are happier than we are. In comparison, the longer we interact face-to-face with friends, the less we think others are happier than we are.[6]

Meanwhile, image-making over time keeps us from living daily in a spirit of transparency. In order to protect ourselves from hurt or simply to impress others, we make it harder for others to know and love us. Ironically, the duplicitous images we create of ourselves undercut the very love and trust we desire from others.

PROJECTING A FALSE VERSUS TRUE SELF

False Self	True Self
Hides	Reveals
Traps	Frees
Protects self	Makes self vulnerable
Keeps people out	Invites people in
Follows lies	Seeks truth
Rejects giftedness	Embraces giftedness
Sabotages trust	Fosters trust

Pope Benedict XVI addresses the topic of self-duplicity in a profound public teaching. In "Truth, Proclamation and Authenticity of Life in the Digital Age," he recognizes the risk of using digital media to construct false social identities. "There exists a Christian way of being present in the digital world: this takes the form of a communication that is honest and open, responsible and respectful of others." He challenges followers of Jesus Christ "to be authentic and faithful, and not give in to the illusion of constructing an artificial public profile for oneself."[7]

By communicating faithfully with God and others, we learn more about who we really are. To fully embrace our true self, we need to become intimate with the Son of God, confirming that we are made in the very image and likeness of our Creator. Regardless of what the media and others tell us, we are God's special, forgiven, redeemed children. We belong to God. Without Christ, our faces become undistinguished expressions of socially constructed personae.

One difficulty with being both authentic and transparent is that we have to face our real, imperfect selves. We can't discover our true self without considering our false self. If we don't face our sinful selves, we can't capture our risen, beloved selves.

Preventing Lies

A wife wondered how her husband could lie to her about something so relatively insignificant. He said he had returned the golf putter he had purchased. But then she spotted it poking out of his golf bag. She began wondering what else he had been hiding from her. She even started wondering if she really knew her own husband.[8] If her husband would lie about minor things, maybe he would deceive her about major things as well.

When we discover that someone has lied to us about even something relatively trivial, we start wondering if they're honest persons. It takes only a few confirmed lies before we start questioning the person's overall character. Pretty soon we don't trust them. In 1972 half of all Americans felt they could trust others. Today one-third of Americans say most people can be trusted. The trend is clear. Beginning with the baby boomers, each generation has entered adulthood less trusting than those who came before them.[9]

Lies are among the most damaging forms of unfaithfulness in interpersonal relationships. When a commercial or a door-to-door salesperson exaggerates particular product claims, we usually just accept it as business. Our expectations are low. When a loved one deceives us, we are hurt if not also angry. We rightly assume that loved ones owe us truthfulness.

A *lie* is a statement intended to deceive. If we say something that we believe to be true but later discover that it wasn't accurate, we haven't lied. We didn't intend to deceive. We simply misspoke. Perhaps we should have known better, but at least we didn't intentionally lead others astray.

According to St. Augustine, a lie has two elements: a divided heart and a will to deceive. A divided heart is an inconsistency between one's mind and expression. A lie is expressing what we know in our heart is not true; it's a calculated attempt to mislead.[10] We deceive God, others, and ourselves when our words and actions are not consistent with what we know to be true. In effect, lying is a kind of moral and spiritual sickness that takes many forms and is sometimes hard to diagnose. Writer Marilyn Chandler McEntyre observes, "Truth-telling is difficult because the varieties of untruth are so many and so well disguised. Lies are hard to identify when they come in the form of apparently innocuous imprecision, socially acceptable slippage, hyperbole masquerading as enthusiasm, or well-placed propaganda."[11]

Some white lies are probably justifiable. *White lies* are those with little moral importance and generally without significant consequences.[12] For instance, we might compliment someone on his or her clothing or cooking even if we don't believe that the fashion or food is particularly good. People often accept such fibs as social niceties. But what if we tell someone that we will pray for him or her even if we (and they) know we probably won't? Is that an acceptable white lie?

We lie for all kinds of reasons, but especially to protect our pride. We deceive others when we are ashamed by our actions and don't want our dark deeds exposed. We feel like we must protect our ego.[13] Our self-esteem is at stake. In fact, we're so accustomed to prideprotecting deception that we even exaggerate our affection for others. Such deception is so routine that when study participants were asked to recall deceptive affections it was not a particularly stressful or anxiety-inducing activity for them. Lying is so commonplace that it seems to produce little or no physiological arousal.[14]

A study asked college students to analyze the veracity of statements in their everyday conversations. The results were amazing: only 38.5 percent of their statements were completely true. Students justified

TEN REASONS WE LIE

1. To protect our pride
2. To hide our destructive actions
3. To save face
4. To circumvent punishment
5. To retain control
6. To exploit others
7. To avoid admitting failure
8. To maintain relational harmony
9. To spare others from expressing their feelings
10. To prevent harm/embarrassment to others and self

their "little white lies" as means of avoiding embarrassment, protecting their image, circumventing tension, and controlling the situation.[15]

Perhaps most amazing of all, we regularly lie to ourselves—even about lying itself! We rationalize lying as a way to protect others even though we generally do it selfishly to protect ourselves. About 76 percent of all lies are told for the benefit of the liar, not the person deceived.[16] So much for justifying most of our lies by pretending that we have good intentions and care more about others than ourselves.

Spreading Gossip

Is anything more secretly delicious than *gossip*—idle talk and rumors about others' intimate lives? What is conversation for, if not hush-hush chatter about other people? "Did you know?" "Did you hear?" "Guess what I discovered!" "Did you see online?" "So and so told me that . . ." "Really!" "Wow!" Gossiping is fun, stimulating, and even cathartic. Don't we feel better about ourselves when we discover what's wrong with others? Between 65 and 90 percent of everyday conversation might be gossip.[17]

When it comes to gossip, we're all like wayward journalists who are less concerned with truthtelling than capturing an audience. Gossip gives us a chance to draw attention to ourselves without talking about ourselves. We get to play news reporter; if we have lots of juicy gossip to spread we can even pretend to be a news anchor. Gossip allows us "to find a perverse enjoyment in somebody else's dilemma."[18] We revel in knowing the intimate details of others' problems and find pleasure in telegraphing this news and demonstrating that we're networked. Also, some gossip is a defense mechanism that helps us preserve our self-esteem by elevating ourselves in the process of tearing others down.[19]

Of course not all secretive talk about others is gossipy chitchat. We also share information about others in order to inform and protect people from those who might take advantage of them. Researchers have found that private talk about people's reputations in the workplace can have at least four benefits: (1) helping us know about and avoid bad people, (2) helping other vulnerable people know about

SEVEN TYPES OF EVIL REPORTERS

1. Backbiter—speaks against absent persons
2. Busybody—seeks out personal information and spreads it like wildfire
3. Complainer—faults others
4. Murmurer—grumbles about another
5. Slanderer—injures others' reputations
6. Talebearer—elaborates to make a story more dramatic
7. Whisperer—talks privately about others to hurt them

Adapted from Michael D. Sedler, *Stop the Runaway Conversation: Take Control over Gossip and Criticism* (Grand Rapids: Chosen, 2001), 80–85.

and avoid bad people, (3) reducing the negative effects of bad people's actions on others, and (4) deterring selfishness and promoting cooperation.[20]

Gossip usually includes bits of truth, but the full truth is always more complicated. Gossip: "So and so is getting a divorce." Response: "Really?" Behind that bit of dramatic gossip might be years of one couple's real-life stories of joy, pain, and separation. It's like TV news: reporters sometimes offer sound bites about complex world events.

For Christians, the line between gossip and even a prayer request can become fairly thin. We have to consider our motives. Are we truly spreading news about others because we care about them and wish the best for them in prayer? Do we really intend to pray for them? Are we careful not to pass along the news to those whom we know tend to gossip more than pray?

Gossip tends to be manipulative and controlling. We use it to gain attention, influence others, and bond with co-gossipers. As we tell a tale, we embellish, exaggerate, and distort the details; we set aside factual truth in favor of a juicy spin. Most gossipers don't highlight the best in others or seek to encourage troubled souls. They implicitly question others' reputations with little regard for the consequences. Whereas love demands that we trust and expect the best in others, gossip suspects and expects the worst.[21]

TEST THE NEED BEFORE SPEAKING

Writer and pastor R. T. Kendall presents a helpful acronym to review before speaking: NEED, based on Jesus's command to "Do to others as you would have them do to you" (Luke 6:31). Simply put, we ask ourselves if our words will truly meet another's *need*. Put to this test, evil reporting would cease.

N—Is what I am about to share *necessary*?
E—Will the information I share *emancipate* (set free) the other?
E—Will the information I share *energize* the other?
D—Will I *dignify* the other by what I am about to say?

Adapted from R. T. Kendall, *Controlling the Tongue*
(Lake Mary, FL: Charisma House, 2007), 175.

A mark of a true friend is secrecy, says twelfth-century English monk Aelred of Rievaulx.[22] Friends are trustworthy confidants. We can tell them personal information and be confident that they will not spread it or use it to hurt or belittle us. Simply put, one can't be both a gossiper and a trustworthy friend. The writer of Proverbs says, "A gossip betrays a confidence, but a trustworthy person keeps a secret."[23]

Truthtelling for Trust

In *Mere Christianity*, C. S. Lewis suggests that a compelling argument for the existence of God is morality, especially moral absolutes that nearly all human beings affirm.[24] He cites the absolute ethical mandate of telling the truth instead of lying. It's hard to imagine anyone believing that lying is, except in rare cases, morally better than telling the truth. Why? Because no one wants to be deceived. We greatly prefer friends, family, and coworkers who are straight with us. And we assume they want to be treated similarly—that we owe truth to each other.

In other words, we adhere to a kind of social contract that truthtelling is better than deception; lying lacks fairness.[25] To put it differently, we believe we are socially obligated not to say what we believe to be false or questionable.[26] When we interact with each other, we normally expect mutual honesty.

Maybe this social contract should apply to our relationships with ourselves as well. Self-deception destroys our relationship with ourselves. The addict who denies such addiction to himself or herself likely destroys the possibility of other honest self-talk. Denial—a form of self-deception—probably erodes one's trust in one's self.

There is a catch, however, when it comes to building trust. The only way to build trust is to dialogue openly and honestly. Yet we're not comfortable doing this until we've built up enough trust with

SCRIPTURE ON TRUTHTELLING

- "Speak the truth to each other" (Zech. 8:16).
- "Put off falsehood and speak truthfully to your neighbor" (Eph. 4:25).
- "No one who practices deceit will dwell in my house; no one who speaks falsely will stand in my presence" (Ps. 101:7).
- "The LORD detests lying lips, but he delights in people who are trustworthy" (Prov. 12:22).
- Jesus is "full of grace and truth" (John 1:14). Our words likewise must be true.

Adapted from David P. Gushee, "The Truth about Deceit: Most Lies Are Pitiful Attempts to Protect Our Pride," *Christianity Today*, March 2006, 68.

each other. So building trust normally is a slow, delicate dance in which partners learn to lead and to follow. It requires reciprocal self-disclosure and ever-deepening intimacy.

In *Why Am I Afraid to Tell You Who I Am?*, priest John Powell writes, "I am afraid to tell you who I am, because, if I tell you who I am, you might not like who I am, and it's all that I have."[27] It's scary to be vulnerable and to invite people into our lives. We may face rejection, create a negative image, or have to admit and then confront our own destructive actions. Yet such honest, open sharing is the only avenue to close, fulfilling relationships. Communication scholar and priest Paul Soukup says, "Self disclosure rests on trust, our willingness to

RISKS AND BENEFITS
OF SELF-DISCLOSURE

Risks
- Rejection
- Alienation
- Negative image
- Loss of control
- Unfortunate consequences

Benefits
- Trust
- Intimacy
- Self-awareness
- Emotional release

Adapted from Lawrence B. Rosenfeld, "Self-Disclosure
Avoidance: Why I Am Afraid to Tell You Who I Am,"
Communication Monographs 46, no. 1 (1979): 63–74.

listen to the voice of another and not to let ourselves become distracted by listening to those other voices that lead to the walls separating Samaritans and Jews, men and women, friends and foes."[28]

Truthtelling Nurtures Shalom

Followers of Jesus Christ are called to speak the truth in love.[29] When we do so, we can expect our relationships to flourish beyond our imagination.

Speaking truth creates trust.

Since forthright talk builds trust, we should seek to be honest with others. When someone realizes we aren't completely truthful, they will begin distrusting us from then on.[30] Simply put, deceit sabotages our authenticity while truthtelling patiently nurtures mutually candid relationships.

Speaking truth shows our faith in others.

When we speak straightforwardly, we show our faith in others by demonstrating our trust in them. Sharing openly and honestly invites others into our lives, allowing them to come alongside us to carry our burdens and care for us—just as we care for them. It nurtures faith that people will be there for each other to listen, learn, and serve. Perhaps Sharon's daughter didn't fully trust her mother because of some earlier episode. Or perhaps her mother didn't trust Sharon and had previously peeked too frequently into her daughter's private life.

Speaking truth demonstrates maturity.

It isn't always comfortable to tell the truth. Truthtelling often requires admitting a wrong, taking responsibility for the offense, and paying the consequences. It involves a willingness to face hard truths that are disappointing and disturbing.[31] Consequences can be considerable—perhaps a lost job, a severed relationship, or a tarnished self-image. Facing the truth requires plenty of maturity by owning up to the consequences for ourselves as well as others.

Speaking truth reunites us with God.

Lying breaks our fellowship with God. It is only through facing and confessing our sins that broken fellowship is restored. Such confession is an opportunity for God's heart to be thrilled by reconciling forgiveness.[32] Moreover, honestly praising God brings us closer to him.

Speaking truth promotes unity.

We are created to dwell together in community, but lying severs our connections with others. When we hide from one another through independent action, fake social identities, or dishonest conversation, we break from unity with others.[33]

Speaking truth allows accountability.

By speaking honestly to each other, we can better hold one another accountable for our actions. We need to be transparent with trusted, devoted, and committed friends who speak the truth in love to us.[34] Accountable people are truthful.

Speaking truth establishes an authentic platform for sharing Christ with others.

As Christians, we are called to share Christ's message of love and hope. God commands us to be faithful to him and to share the true gospel. Others rightly assume that we speak the truth and that our actions reflect our convictions. When our words and our lives are out of sync, people will call into question our integrity, which greatly hinders our Christian witness.

Conclusion

In our scientific age we tend to think of truth merely as factuality. From a biblical perspective, truth is also faithfulness—it's "being true" to others, including God, neighbor, and self. Lying destroys trust and thereby weakens relationships. By contrast, being true to one another nurtures trust and builds lasting relationships. Honesty and transparency help us to flourish with others in community. "Truth is not simply something that is believed or even spoken. Rooted in faith in the trustworthy Triune God, truth is a way of being, a path that is followed, and a place that one inhabits," writes ethics professor David Gushee.[35]

On a crisp autumn afternoon, Sharon's daughter decided to hide behind her text messages. She constructed the illusion that her life was good when it was actually falling apart. How different the story could have unfolded if Sharon's daughter openly answered her mother's questions, sharing her deepest struggles and doubts in life. Such honesty would have offered Sharon the opportunity to be a genuine and faithful friend in her daughter's difficult journey toward healing. Fortunately, they both discovered the truth and stepped out in faith to restart their communication and rebuild their relationship.

In the next chapter we show how important encouragement is for building each other up personally and in community. Encouragement from God and others gives us the courage to face difficult communication situations, to keep going faithfully in the midst of adversity, disappointment, and suffering. When trust wanes in our relationships, we need plenty of encouragement to persevere.

6

ENCOURAGE OTHERS

In the movie *The Pursuit of Happyness*, the father, played by Will Smith, stifles his son's dream of becoming a professional basketball player: "You'll excel at a lot of things, just not this." But after realizing the crushing impact of his disheartening remark, the father adds, "Don't let anybody tell you that you can't do something—not even me. . . . You want something, go out and get it."[1]

For aspiring writer Russell Baker, who became a *New York Times* columnist, encouragement came from an English teacher who read his essay to the entire class. "For the first time, light shone on a possibility," remembers Baker about that event. "In the eleventh grade, at the eleventh hour as it were, I had discovered a calling. It was the happiest moment of my entire school career. . . . Mr. Fleagle had opened a door for me."[2]

Encouraging words open opportunities for us. They inspire us to try something new, to excel at a talent, to offer and accept forgiveness, to love others and ourselves, to see ourselves in a new, more promising light. Encouraging words are like hugs of hope. And they don't require lengthy discourse. Some of the best encouragement is like a heartening, unexpected text message that says "thanks for being a friend." It's the quality, not the quantity of words that best encourages others.

As we explain in this chapter, we live in a society loaded with discouraging words that suffocate hope. By contrast, even small amounts of encouragement hearten us and give us courage to move forward even in dispiriting times. When we encourage others we (1) affirm them, (2) exhort (persuade) them to live faithfully, (3) model for them the life of faith, and (4) accompany them through discouraging times. If we are encouraging someone we know well and see frequently, we essentially walk with them during their discouraging days. There are times when we need to encourage ourselves too. This chapter makes clear that flattery typically does not help—it merely boosts our egos instead of warming our hearts. Real friends regularly offer and receive the kind of encouragement that can produce successful basketball players and newspaper columnists.

Getting Discouraged

In a world of broken relationships and failed efforts, we all suffer *dis*-couragement. Couples divorce. Roommates employ the silent treatment. Older siblings mutter at younger ones. Coworkers jealously protect their emotional turf to prove their own worth. Former friends seek revenge rather than forgiveness. People are born to trouble as surely as sparks fly upward from a fire, says the writer of the book of Job.[3] That's life in a world where we cocoon and criticize. It can be terribly disheartening.

So sometimes we lose confidence in ourselves and trust in others—even God. We wonder: "Where was the Holy Spirit when I said something terribly inappropriate to a friend?" "Why didn't I listen better to a relative who was depressed or suicidal?" "How could I give such a lousy interview for a job I really wanted, especially when I prayed and prepped so hard?" We try to reach out to others but are ignored. We long to be part of a group but are left out. Sometimes we get so dispirited that we question whether our relationships with God and others are worth the effort. "Whatever!"

We turn on the TV or surf the internet to take our minds off of our discouragement.

It especially hurts when people say things that we rightly or wrongly interpret as personal criticism. They may even speak up without realizing the full punch of their words—like the father's first dismissive words to his son in *The Pursuit of Happyness*. If we're particularly sensitive at the time, others' comments don't have to be overly nasty

---

QUESTIONS AND STATEMENTS WITH IMPLIED CRITICISMS

- "Are we out of milk again?" ("You can't even manage this simple task!")
- "Have you started job hunting?" ("You're so lazy!")
- "You should have easily won that race." ("You're not trying hard enough.")
- "Maybe you shouldn't wear that dress." ("You'll embarrass me.")
- "How's the diet going?" ("You're gaining weight.")

---

to inflict emotional pain. Even their mildly critical language seems to imply that we have little value.[4] Still, harshly delivered, disrespectful words are the worst; they can crush our spirits for days or weeks. Verbally abusive parents can negatively affect their children's self-identities for years into adulthood.

Sometimes criticism is implied in a seemingly joking manner—like in a sitcom one-liner meant to elicit a camera-ready reaction shot from the recipient of the attack. In fact, sitcoms often are based on put-downs because the remarks strike the viewer as humorous, and the humor seems to blunt the full impact of the remark just enough to keep audiences from feeling that the recipient was treated indignantly.

We all know that disapproval generally stings more than reassurance heals. Even mild criticism can hurt us deeply. We live in webs of overt and covert criticism that constantly remind us that we don't measure up to others' expectations. For every teaspoon of discouragement we probably need a glass of encouragement, or we begin to lose heart. Walt Disney said that there are three types of people: *well-poisoners* are discouragers; *lawn mowers* are self-absorbed (taking care only of their own lawns); and *life-enhancers* are inspiring, reaching out to enrich the lives of others.[5]

To gauge how much discouragement you offer others, try committing for one day to not saying (including texting, blogging, emailing, or tweeting) anything negative about anyone—direct or implied. Don't say anything unkind about anyone the next day either; don't even give unkind looks. After doing this for a day or two, can you go an entire week without speaking negatively toward someone?

Courageously Keeping Heart

It takes virtue, especially courage, to forge ahead in the midst of discouragement. The word "courage" comes from the Latin *cor* for "heart" or "spirit." Courage is all about how we keep heart while experiencing disappointments and hardships. Courage is far more than onetime acts of heroism in seemingly impossible situations. Courage addresses our attitudes and actions in everyday life as we face uncertainty, such as going on a first date, starting a new school program, interviewing for a job, or attending a group like Alcoholics Anonymous for the first time.

A courageous parent continues nurturing a child until that child can become a more independent adult. A brave friend stays with us through thick and thin. A bold teacher goes back to the classroom day after day to serve the students.

An encourager is the kind of person who regularly and genuinely gives others heart in the course of daily tasks and relationships. For instance, most of us will remember a teacher who routinely encouraged us more than we will remember the subject matter that teacher taught. A great instructor models encouragement by encouraging students. Every station in life is a place for giving and receiving such grace-filled encouragement.

Courage isn't weak. We're courageous when we admit and deal with reality rather than withdraw from it or pretend it doesn't exist. Relational reality can involve everything from daily difficulties to physical and emotional pain. Often we face relational fears—fears of rejection, abandonment, and failure. We doubt our own abilities. We need courage to move ahead in hope.

We *en*-courage the hearts of others by giving them the courage they need to go on in life even in the midst of frustrations, hardships, and disappointments. We encourage people by giving them the hope and confidence they need for daily living as well as for specific, more challenging situations. An abused wife needs the courage to speak up to her husband and to those who will stand beside her as she seeks to stop or escape from the abuse. A depressed friend needs courage to keep going in dark times.

Think of encouragement in terms of verbal and nonverbal support for our neighbors in need—which includes just about everyone we know and interact with. We can try to live independently, but we can't flourish without neighborly encouragers. We will flourish only when we receive lots of loving encouragement. The message of support is, "Take heart, you're not alone; I am with you."

Giving Heart to Others

Jesus repeatedly offers heartfelt encouragement. For instance, he uses variations on "fear not" or "do not be afraid" over one hundred times in the Bible. Ministering to the early church, the apostle Paul frequently offers this gift. His words directed Christians to be strong and to wait upon the Lord.[6] He reminds Jesus's followers that everything will work out just as God has ordained.[7] Like Paul, we're called to bless others by encouraging them. There are at least four scriptural patterns for encouragement—affirming, exhorting, modeling, and accompanying others.

Encouraging by Affirming

First, we encourage by affirming. The New Testament suggests that encouragers are like a construction crew.[8] Encouragers build others up not just for the occasional big challenges but also for everyday dwelling in the world. We communicate the comforting, relationship-building,

Six Ways to Affirm Others

1. Speak honest, heartfelt words of praise. ("You know, you're really good at that.")
2. Express appreciation. ("You're so thoughtful.")
3. Listen attentively. ("I hear you.")
4. Acknowledge them. ("It's great to see you.")
5. Credit their contributions. ("You raise a wonderful point!")
6. Speak well of them in front of their peers. ("Luke was terrific in that role.")

foundational love of God through our own love of others. As some biblical translations put it, we "edify" others so that they can discharge everyday duties; this kind of encouragement comforts.[9]

Practically speaking, we shouldn't hesitate to lavish others with honest, affirming words. We should pay attention to others—let them know we are trying to understand how they feel—by attentively listening, without judgment. We should acknowledge others, even with just a smile if we can't find the appropriate words. We should sincerely praise them. We should craft words that rightly help them feel good about themselves. We ought to tell friends and family how much they mean to us. And we should compliment them in front of others.

Columnist Russell Baker's teacher affirmed his gift for writing and in only a few words gave him the courage to pursue a particular career. How many of us have particular skills that even we don't know we could use to serve others? Without encouragers, we might never discover them.

On the flip side, we need to avoid tearing down others through our clumsy or inappropriate interactions. After all, we know from our own lives how devastating implicitly negative comments can be; even mild criticism can come across to others as shouting to the entire world that they have little value in our sight.[10]

Long-term encouragement or discouragement makes a significant difference in relationships. For instance, what parents say to their adolescent during the middle school years is critically important.

FIVE THINGS NOT TO SAY TO YOUR FRIEND ABOUT GAINING WEIGHT

1. "You've put on a little weight"—as if he or she doesn't know it already.
2. "You shouldn't be eating that"—as if you are the diet police.
3. "Haven't you had enough?"—as if you should monitor portions.
4. "It's easy, all you have to do is . . ."—as if you know how to lose weight.
5. "I'm just trying to help"—as if you really know how to help.

Adapted from Cynthia Sass, "Things NOT to Say to Your Partner about Losing Weight," Health.com, http://news.health.com/2014/01/31/5-things-not-to-say-to-your-partner-about-weight-loss/.

Poor teenage self-esteem is linked to everything from depression and anxiety to eating disorders. In contrast, parents' words of recognition and acceptance foster young adults' mental health and well-being.[11] Moreover, parents' positive communication with adolescents creates open and honest relationships across the generations. When parents affirm their teenagers, the offspring tend to encourage their parents.[12] Both generations flourish.

The bottom line is that people who encourage others tend to receive kind words of support in return. If we want to hear soul-refreshing affirmation from others, we should affirm them. We tend to reap the affirmation we sow. If we surround ourselves with critical, cynical people, we'll feel discouraged. Real friends are mutual encouragers. To be encouraged, choose friends who are encouragers. Then affirm them too.

In a high-tech world, written notes of encouragement are particularly effective. Who in your life needs a bit of encouragement? Write them a note expressing your appreciation for them. For more impact, send a handwritten note in a card rather than an email or text message. Also, speak well of them to friends and family members—let them overhear your honest praise.

Encouraging by Exhorting

Second, we encourage by calling others to live faithfully. We give hope by tangibly persuading them to live in the Lord. In other words, we don't encourage just by affirming others with our appropriate hugs and words; we also encourage them through *exhortative encouragement* by gently persuading them to live with the hope of Jesus Christ in a broken world. The New Testament language suggests that exhorting is like preaching—but not necessarily preachy.[13]

Think of exhortation this way: we all know people who are doing things that are not in their own best relational interests. And the same could be said of us. So what do we do about it? Do we just comfort one another from the sidelines, pretending that all is well when we're clearly living outside of God's will? Or do we also lovingly try to sway each other to seek better, more enriching relationships with God and one another?

None of us likes to be surrounded with self-righteous, preachy people. That's not the point of mutual exhortation. Instead we should be the kinds of friends that humbly coax each other to do what's in our mutual best interests as followers of Jesus Christ. Interpersonal exhortation reminds us that God too is on our side and that we should be on his side. There is no better way to deep encouragement than being friends with friends of Jesus Christ.

Exhortative encouragement is difficult to share even with intimate friends. Obviously we don't want to come across as holier-than-thou nags. We need to respect others, granting them the emotional space to be themselves and make their own decisions. Moreover, we shouldn't hypocritically tell others to do things that we don't do. We have to earn the right to exhort by getting our own house in order. This is why such exhortative encouragement often requires real friendship; trustworthy friends typically have earned the respect to counsel one another.

If your communication is dripping with criticisms and complaints, others are likely to turn a deaf ear when honest correction is warranted. In contrast, if you continually offer heartfelt praise and show care for others, then when *admonition* (loving correction) is warranted, you've already earned a *platform* (a place of honor and respect) so that others will listen and seriously consider your comments.

Moreover, if someone warrants a complaint or correction, we shouldn't begin the conversation critically. The apostle Paul didn't; he even began some of his most critical letters with thanksgiving.[14] It can take the heart right out of us when the first thing we hear in the morning or when we arrive at work is criticism. Regardless of how others act, we should begin with a smile and a compliment—even something as simple as "Good morning!" or "Great to see you." If we can't think of anything positive to say about someone else, we've got a problem. Is there no goodness in someone else? Who are we kidding, except ourselves?

Perhaps in today's world, where religion seems so phony and hypocritical to many people, we should exhort through invitation rather

---

SEVEN THINGS NOT TO SAY TO SOMEONE WITH ANXIETY

1. "Don't sweat the small stuff." (What's small to you might not be to them.)
2. "Calm down." (If the person could have simply calmed down, they would have already done so.)
3. "Just do it." (Empathy, not tough love, is most assuring to them.)
4. "Everything is going to be fine." (Chances are, they know that there is no simple fix and such a blanket statement doesn't help.)
5. "I'm stressed out too." (Real anxiety is nothing like mere stress.)
6. "Have a drink—it'll take your mind off of it." (A drink might make your friend feel better in the short run, but it can make anxiety worse in the long run.)
7. "Did I do something wrong?" (Don't take your friend's anxiety personally. Be his or her friend.)

Adapted from Lindsay Holmes, "Seven Things You Shouldn't Say to Someone with Anxiety," *Huffington Post*, February 2, 2014, http://www.huffingtonpost.com/2014/02/17/things-not-to-say-to-some_n_4781182.html.

than proclamation. In other words, we might think of encouraging exhortation as persuading by inviting each other to have greater faith and to live out that faith more completely—not by telling people exactly what to feel or do. We can love others by inviting them to be faithful to the God who calls them—a welcoming that mirrors God's calling of his followers to faithfulness. As inviters, we winsomely point others to God rather than to ourselves. We encourage others in ways that draw them nearer to God. We urge people forward in their faith,[15] even as we humbly acknowledge our own weaknesses.

Encouraging by Modeling Action

Third, we encourage through our concrete actions that model hope. The biblical figure Barnabas is a great example. Barnabas, whose name means "son of encouragement," gave life to the discouraged by selling his land to benefit others. Barnabas's generosity encouraged the young church to continue in its mission.[16] He stood up for Saul (Paul) amid rejection by the apostles,[17] and he stood up for John Mark despite opposition from Paul.[18]

John Mark had abandoned Barnabas and Paul on their first missionary journey. Even so, Barnabas faithfully took John Mark under his wings, graciously giving him a second chance to show his faithfulness. We similarly encourage when we model courage.

Long before Walt Disney's fame, writes his daughter Diane Disney Miller, individuals walked beside her dad to encourage him during his early years as an artist. "When things seemed blackest," she recalls, a dentist asked her father to create an animated cartoon teaching children to take care of their teeth. When it was time to meet and seal the deal, Walt told the dentist that he was unable to meet with him. "Why?" the dentist asked. Walt replied, "I haven't any shoes . . ." and went on to explain that his shoes were "falling apart and I left them at the shoemakers. He won't let me have them until I can dig up a dollar and a half." The dentist paid the shoemaker, an act of kindness signifying his confidence in Walt's potential as an artist.[19]

We encourage partly by demonstrating the courage of our own convictions. We model encouragement to others by living encouraging lives. Our lives suggest to others whether or not we have any reasons for hope. Our lives can say to others, "You too can live expectantly. Take heart. Be encouraged."

The ancient Greek philosopher Aristotle said that communicators should use "all available means of persuasion" at their disposal to persuade others.[20] We could add that as followers of Jesus Christ we should use all of the ways available to encourage others. Encouragement is much more than a matter or manner of speech. God calls us to touch, smile, listen, and text hopefulness. But perhaps most important of all, how we live speaks volumes about our reasons for hope amid a discouraging world littered with broken relationships.

Encouraging by Accompanying Others

Fourth, we encourage when we empathize with the disheartened and accompany them through difficult times. If our hearts are open, we can become others' companions in the ups and downs of life. In scriptural terms, we can become others' *paracletes*—advocates called to their sides.

An anxious colleague faced with a possible layoff needs to know that there are people who will stay with him or her through the fearful weeks or months ahead. To a large extent, ministry is all about walking encouragingly with others through the valleys as well as the hills of life. Encouragers walk with us. Discouragers eventually walk away.

These four means of encouraging others show that our best expressions of encouragement flow not from a sense of legalistic duty or burdensome obligation but from a genuine sense of delight.[21] We learn to enjoy offering honest praise, exhorting others to live faithfully, modeling encouragement, and walking alongside others facing discouragement. We delight in their hope just as much as in our own.

In fact, we delight in everyone else's encouragement. We don't encourage only individuals who are like us, agree with us, share our faith, or are close to us. We're not in a position to curse those who do not share our faith;[22] rather, we should affirm the likeness of God in them.[23] For us, encouragement is a way of life worth sharing with all of our neighbors—with every discouraged person. Why shouldn't we offer a word of thanks to a salesclerk or restaurant server who took care of us? Why shouldn't we see all of our connections with others as opportunities to encourage?

Herman Miller CEO Max De Pree got a letter that was addressed to

Max De Pree
Author of *Dear Zoe*
Holland, Michigan

De Pree was so amazed that he had received the letter from a reader of his book that he called the postmaster to offer thanks. The postmaster told him, "We find about 100 letters like this a week that we have to do some special work on to get them delivered." Then he added, "You're the first person who ever called to say thank you."[24] How could that be the case, especially in a city dotted with churches? Do we take one another for granted that much? Do we assume that if someone is getting paid they don't need or deserve heartfelt encouragement?

Seeking Encouragement for Ourselves

We should also seek encouragement for our own hearts. The more we are encouraged, the more capacity we have to encourage others. Everyone needs it.

One of the leaders of the Protestant Reformation, John Calvin, "never ceased to feel his need of encouragement; never ceased to seek it in the Lord; never ceased to find it; and so was always able to comfort others with the same comfort wherewith he himself was comforted of God."[25] One reason Calvin might have needed such significant encouragement was that he was not always a nice man. At times he was intolerant toward and even persecuted those who disagreed with him. He must have had doubts about his actions in spite of his own courage. He was human, sin and all. Often some of the most influential and seemingly successful people need considerable encouragement in the face of their public and private failures.

When we overly draw on our own abilities to build ourselves up, and when friends and family seem too distressed to encourage us, we can discover afresh the power of God's reassurance by appealing directly to Jesus Christ. Scripture is the story of God's grace in the midst of human fear and disobedience. The Psalms, for instance, portray life realistically as despair and disappointment, but they usually end in words of praise and thanksgiving for a personal God who keeps his people safe from the pit of despair. The gospel is the

ENCOURAGEMENT FROM THE BOOK OF PSALMS

The LORD is close to the brokenhearted
  and saves those who are crushed in spirit.
The righteous person may have many troubles,
  but the LORD delivers him from them all.

Psalm 34:18–19

ultimate encouragement for those drowning in discouragement. The good news is that God does for us what we can't do for ourselves. This is why we can call upon enough strength and encouragement in the Lord to share with others.

One intended beauty of fellowship is spending time together with encouragers who help us to live with joy and delight. Seek friends who are the kinds of persons you would like to be—namely, a blessing to others. They will encourage you, and you will encourage them and others.

Fending Off Flattery

Unfortunately, much encouragement is phony and even selfish: (1) we encourage out of obligation rather than genuine gratitude, (2) we encourage others so they will feel good about us, carefully avoiding any exhortative language, and (3) we partner with someone to offer each other mutually flowery compliments that we both know are exaggerated. All three can be signs of foolish flattery.

Scripture distinguishes between encouragement and *flattery*—excessive compliments usually meant to ingratiate us to others.

Whereas a true encourager has others' best interests in mind—including encouraging them honestly—a flatterer typically has self-interest in mind. The encouragers' expressions are sincere, while the flatterer aims to impress and to gain favor.[26] Encouragers use affirming words to build up others' spirits, whereas flatterers use such language to disarm recipients and sometimes even to spring a trap to take advantage of them.[27]

True encouragement doesn't require that others reciprocate or that we gain something personally from encouraging them. Like all grace, genuine encouragement is a gift, given freely. Others may or may not reciprocate—that's their choice. Of course others will tend to reciprocate over time by encouraging those who encourage them. But encouragement doesn't require or even demand a response. The recipient doesn't have to say "thank you" or return a compliment. There should be no strings attached when we hearten another, since this is our opportunity simply to express love, period.[28]

Reciprocal flattery can be mutually debilitating even as two friends knowingly celebrate their lies about one another. Encouragement demands that we humbly offer honest praise for people; otherwise, we may be promoting warm and fuzzy feelings but failing to foster godly character and neglecting to hold one another accountable.[29] Humility in particular makes our encouragement genuine.[30] It diverts attention from us and gives it to others based on their need for truth as well as praise.

Given the dangers of flattery, is too much encouragement a bad thing? Will excessive encouragement turn recipients into self-glorifying, prideful, and arrogant persons? Perhaps this happens sometimes, but not if the encouragement is free of flattery and appropriate to the situation. Besides, it's far more likely that excessive discouragement will lead to others' sense of rejection and defeat. When it comes to authentic encouragement, few people receive enough.

Harvard Business Review reported that the most important factor in business "effectiveness"—defined by financial performance, customer satisfaction, and feedback ratings of team members—was the ratio of positive comments (e.g., "I agree with that" or "That's a terrific idea") to negative comments (e.g., "I don't agree with you" or "We shouldn't even consider doing that" or those that are even more sarcastic and disparaging). The top-performing groups used about five positive comments for every negative one. The lowest-performing teams averaged about three negative comments to each positive one. Of course, some negative feedback is important as groups evaluate their work, but it doesn't take much negativity to bring down the performance.[31]

Conclusion

Encouraging language and smiles come more easily to extroverted individuals with strong self-esteem. Also, some of us even have the benefit of growing up in families where parents modeled many forms of encouragement. In any case, we all have room to grow as we learn to speak blessings to others.[32]

We can cultivate the virtue of being an encourager by becoming ever more aware of the goodness in others. One way to accomplish this is to set aside time weekly to review a list of friends, family, and colleagues and remind yourself how they have blessed you and others. Then add to that open contemplation a growing sensitivity to their needs. Recognizing their needs will help motivate you to care and to compliment without any reciprocal expectations. Finally, give praise to God for these people and ask Jesus to walk with and encourage them. These simple practices, anchored in contemplation and prayer, will transform you into a heartfelt encourager. As Christian psychologists Larry Crabb and Dan Allender put it, "Encouragement is more than acquiring a new set of skills. It is the fruit of a self-examined heart and a compassionate, discerning sensitivity to the needs of others."[33]

Encouragement is like fertilizer, water, and sunlight for plants. It nurtures life and hope in people. Our encouragement can inspire a young child to pursue her or his dreams, from sports to journalism. It can provide hope and comfort to the hurting. It can keep the defeated in the game. Ultimately, with the Spirit's help, it can draw others closer to God as they see the love and encouragement of Christ in us. "The LORD is close to the brokenhearted and saves those who are crushed in spirit," writes the psalmist.[34] "He heals the brokenhearted and binds up their wounds."[35] We may be the very person whom God calls to bind up others' wounds. We might even be that person whose heart cries out for hope. Sometimes all it takes is timely and sincere encouragement, even just a few words. Sometimes a text message can mean a lot to a discouraged recipient, especially when the two cannot meet in person. If we have time for texting, we have time for encouraging others.

In the next chapter we address the inevitable conflicts that arise in interpersonal relationships even among friends who encourage each other. Not all conflict is relationally destructive, but ignoring conflicts usually worsens them. So we need the heart and skills to face most conflicts for the sake of building great relationships. In the biblical vision, relationships thrive not merely through the absence of conflict, however, but also through the pursuit of *shalom*—peace and justice.

7

PROMOTE PEACE

David and Nancy divorced after six years of marriage. They continued living in different rooms of the same house because they couldn't find a buyer. They argued over things like who got to park in the garage. They also dealt with awkward silence. Eventually they settled into a semitolerable routine that included watching television at opposite ends of the house.[1]

Their accommodations were unusual, but we all live in imperfect relationships. When most of us begin a relationship we assume that our communication skills are above average and things will work out. For some, however, destructive conflicts spiral, rapport dissolves, and relationships die.

Perhaps David and Nancy could have saved their marriage if they had learned the necessary communication skills to better manage conflicts. Then again, maybe they needed to be more virtuous people and aspire to the qualities associated with the fruit of the Spirit, including gentleness, patience, and self-control. Considering all of their conflict, however, could they really have regained the joy of each other's company?

The biblical view of healthy relationships is much more than the absence of conflict. Scripture's vision is a deeper peace in which people find joy and delight in right relations. This ancient Hebrew vision of right relationships, called *shalom*, is a combination of proper justice and fulfilling peace. It imagines relationships as God's gifts to his image bearers so that they might live in the kind of harmony represented by the garden of Eden, before humans' fall from grace. The further our relationships move away from shalom, the more conflict-ridden they become.

In this chapter we show how to address interpersonal conflicts in ways that will nurture relationships marked by shalom. After first examining the nature of conflict, we go on to explain that, contrary to popular opinion, healthy relationships are not based on the absence of all conflict, on complete agreement, or on thoroughly comfortable communication. Conflicts can present opportunities to listen to each other, to reconsider the quality of our relationships, and to examine how we really view and treat one another. Next, we look closely at shalom as the relational ideal, particularly in terms of peace and justice. We then describe essential *virtues* (good qualities of character) that equip us to seek shalom together, such as being gentle, inviting, cooperative, and mild-mannered persons. Finally, we suggest that cultural, racial, and other differences often are openings for mutual growth. When we address conflicts well, we offer glimpses of the kingdom of God on earth and in heaven.

Examining Conflicts

All relationships produce conflicts, but interpersonal conflicts can be heart-wrenching. In fact, the people we work with most closely, worship with most joyfully, and love most dearly are usually the ones with whom we will have some of our worst, relationship-challenging conflicts. Intimacy breeds both delight and dispute.

The word "conflict" comes from the idea of "striking together." It suggests a battle. Real conflict isn't just disagreement, since people can agree to amiably disagree. *Interpersonal conflict* is the kind of battle in which people "strike" each other with silence, words, or

THREE WAYS OF TREATING OTHERS

1. The *low road*—where we treat others worse than they treat us
2. The *middle road*—where we treat others the same as they treat us
3. The *high road*—where we treat others better than they treat us

Adapted from John C. Maxwell, *Winning with People: Discover the People Principles That Work for You Every Time* (Nashville: Nelson, 2004), 221.

other actions because of sharp disagreements or misunderstandings. Conflict is relationship-challenging disagreement in action, the nonphysical version of combat. No wonder people often call interpersonal conflicts "fights." "We had a fight last night" means something like "We suffered through an emotional, destructive argument last night."

Conflict differs from simple disagreements in five important ways.

Interpersonal conflicts involve personal differences of value.

Simple disagreements become conflicts when they address overriding principles that can affect decision making. Disagreeing over what time to arrive at the airport for check-in, for instance, is not the same as arguing about why one's spouse is "always late." The latter involves overriding feelings and understandings about a person—even evaluating a person's actions based on a principle of timeliness. Principled people can get into conflicts when their tight standards are more important than their relationships.

Interpersonal conflicts are emotionally charged.

Conflicts have a sharp edge. They bite hearts. They hurt. They're personal. This is why they can ignite a desire to get even. They can be so psychologically overwhelming that we have difficulty thinking clearly. Our communication becomes an emotional burden. In such a case we are faced with the choice of using words to reduce or fuel the conflict. Our tongues can ease or worsen the burdens we bear.[2]

Interpersonal conflicts last for a while.

Conflicts are not onetime disagreements or temporary relational irritations. They represent a pattern of arguing or stonewalling—or both.[3] Often similar issues and language come up repeatedly. After a while, a minor disagreement can explode into yet another "same-old" conflict. Even if earlier conflicts seemed to be resolved, the previous hurt can reemerge in later disputes. When the negative feelings associated with conflicts fester, they shape how each person feels about the other one and the relationship. Whatever two people repeatedly fight about says a lot about the nature of their relationship.

Interpersonal conflicts affect our quality of life.

Conflicts don't just make or break relationships; they affect people's overall quality of life.[4] They impact the everyday ways we treat and talk to each other, what we think about, how well we rest and work, and how well we interact with God. Conflicts affect our ability to enjoy each other's company, to truly care about and support one another. Often only the worst conflicts totally destroy relationships, but recurring conflicts shape the emotional and spiritual atmosphere in which we live.

Interpersonal conflicts affect our credibility as followers of Christ.

For good or bad, the way we handle conflict is a significant part of our witness to those around us. Cross-cultural expert Duane Elmer says that when conflict is "replaced with wholeness and unity," the "power of the Gospel" is released.[5] Conflicts are an opportunity for God's glory to be revealed through our lives. By contrast, nasty, public conflicts hinder our ability to be salt and light to others.

NINE WAYS NOT TO CONFRONT PEOPLE

1. Out of personal irritation and anger
2. Without knowing all of the relevant facts
3. With a judgmental attitude
4. With condemnatory language
5. With an adversarial tone
6. With Scripture as a "club" to clobber others
7. With purely human expectations
8. In the midst of a broken relationship
9. With the expectation of instantaneous progress

Adapted from Paul David Tripp, *War of Words: Getting to the Heart of Your Communication Struggles* (Phillipsburg, NJ: P&R, 2000), 137–38.

Interpersonal conflicts can emerge through social media as well as in-person interactions.

The jury is still out on whether people's use of social media tends to worsen existing interpersonal conflicts, but clearly social-media use requires special care to avoid conflicts escalating from mere misunderstanding. Between 25 and 50 percent of residential college students carry on long-distance dating relationships, often with friends from back home. To cultivate such relationships, the couples need to work hard at sharing openly and honestly with each other.[6] Ironically, the many different ways of communicating (e.g., cell, text, email, chat, video, tweeting) may create more opportunities for failed expectations, heightening the potential for conflict.[7]

Considering Myths about Conflicts

Being human means having the remarkable ability for *metacommunication*—communication about communication. This book is an example of metacommunication. When coworkers discuss how to work together on a presentation, they're metacommunicating.

One benefit of metacommunication is that we can discuss how to identify and manage conflicts. We aren't programmed to repeat the same communication patterns over and over again—like the character played by Bill Murray in *Groundhog Day* or Drew Barrymore in *50 First Dates.*

A downside of metacommunication, however, is that we can generate interpersonal conflicts about conflicts! Sometimes we go on and on, seemingly forever arguing about arguing. Again, communication skills are not always sufficient to address such situations. The state of our hearts is critically important. We have to desire to get beyond the argumentative reruns.

Because interpersonal conflicts are so common and people do talk about them a lot, it seems that everyone has opinions about them— what they are, what causes them, how to solve them, and more. As a result, we tend to hold to particular myths about conflict that limit our metacommunication about resolving real conflicts.

Myth #1—*All conflict is relationally destructive.*

Actually, most conflicts can be openings for people to get to know each other better and learn both to respect one another and to negotiate differences without cocooning or criticizing. Conflicts can help us set agendas for improving relationships. They can highlight possible cultural differences. They can lead us to begin really listening to each other, without agendas. In fact, much marital counseling is designed to do just that. Moreover, conflicts often are clues about larger emotional problems that need to be addressed. Frequently conflicts over sex, for instance, actually point to the broader issue of emotional intimacy.

Myth #2—*Conflicts are entirely preventable.*

There are only two ways to prevent interpersonal conflicts. One is to live like a hermit. Philosopher Richard Kraut writes, "Having no social relations at all with other human beings will eliminate the problem of negative social emotions, but there is a better solution

. . . to have affectionate and nonconflictual relationships with other people—relationships in which one feels warmly toward others and that seldom, if ever, give one reason to be angry or jealous."[8] That's a tall order, but it beats being a loner.

The other way to prevent conflicts is to give in to others' wishes and demands and avoid any lasting convictions or opinions about anything—like an emotional chameleon that changes colors to fit in with the environment.[9] Of course this too is entirely unrealistic. Even the most gifted and skilled communicators can't avert all conflicts simply by relenting to others' demands or accepting their criticisms. True reconciliation can't be imposed by the stronger of two sides.[10]

Christians believe from Scripture that wherever two or more are gathered, Jesus is also present. That's reassuring given that conflict will also be present, both among the gathered believers and between each of them and God. But even following Jesus won't prevent interpersonal conflicts; some of the worst conflicts arise in churches. Christians can end up in church-splitting disagreements over how to pray, worship, and evangelize. Arguments over musical style alone have divided congregations. Perhaps there is more conflict in some churches than in many other social institutions because the stakes seem so high; both sides can believe that they are right with God.

Myth #3—Conflicts are purely emotional.

Actually, psychological distress can impact us physically.[11] Emotionally charged conflicts can cause illness; stress, in particular, lowers our immunity to illness. Science links severe emotional strain, especially post-traumatic stress, to many of the body's physical systems. People in emotionally intensive and deeply interpersonal professions—such as pastors, counselors, nurses, and missionary workers—are often particularly susceptible. Physical, emotional, and probably spiritual dimensions of health are all intimately related.

As communication professor Tim Muehlhoff says, we shouldn't deny or suppress emotions during conflicts. For one thing, it's impossible to be completely unemotional because we're emotional creatures. For another, emotions can motivate us to resolve conflict in order to build stronger relationships. In addition, emotions can remind us that we care about each other and that God cares about us. Finally, Jesus Christ is a personal God of emotions, and we're made in his image.[12] Muehlhoff writes, "The difference between an amicable resolution and a long-lasting feud is, in part, our ability to manage our emotions in the heat of the moment."[13]

Myth #4—Verbal conflict is far less relationally significant than physical conflict.

Words can sting for life. Verbal abuse, in particular, is vastly under-rated as the source of relationship-destroying conflict passed from generation to generation. Some families live together in emotional terror because of the ways members use language like a knife to pierce each other's hearts. When victims of spousal infidelity hear the bad news, they are often shell-shocked. Some therapists treat such victims

---

SIX WAYS TO WORSEN A FRIEND'S SHAME

Everyone feels a degree of shame for things they've said and done. How we respond when someone confides in us about the cause of his or her shame is critically important. Here are responses to avoid:

1. Gasp and confirm how horrified they should be. ("You should feel terrible.")
2. Respond with sympathy. ("Oh, you poor thing.")
3. Demand them to be your pillar of strength. ("You've let me down.")
4. Scold them. ("How could you let this happen?")
5. Refuse to acknowledge they did such a thing. ("You're exaggerating; everybody loves you.")
6. Seek the opportunity to one-up them. ("That's nothing; listen to what I did.")

Adapted from Brené Brown, *The Gifts of Imperfection: Let Go of Who You Think You're Supposed to Be and Embrace Who You Are* (Center City, MN: Hazelden, 2010), 10–11.

like war casualties or hurricane victims and offer post-traumatic stress debriefings.[14] Words of contempt are especially destructive; they can produce lasting shame.[15]

Some Christians have great difficulty accepting Jesus's forgiveness because of the ways that friends and relatives have heaped disapproval on them. Deep shame is one of the most difficult human emotions to overcome; it robs us of the true knowledge that we're created in the image and likeness of God and prevents us from experiencing the deeper joy of Jesus's forgiveness. Physical and verbal abuse can destroy relationships.

Flourishing in Shalom

What are the alternatives to conflict? Some people believe that the alternative is to minimize conflict by properly managing it. A biblical alternative is to be the kinds of persons who are far less likely to create negative conflict.

Rabbi Abraham Heschel says that faithful living requires us to understand and accept our responsibility toward others. He suggests that there are two divergent ways of relating to each other: *manipulation*, which leads to relational death, and *appreciation*, which leads to relational life. When we irresponsibly aim to exploit others, our words become "tools," and each of our relationships becomes a one-way means for getting what we ourselves want from others. By contrast, says Heschel, true human "fellowship depends upon appreciation."[16]

Heschel adds, "We must strive to maintain a balance of power and mercy, of truth and generosity." To be a person is to "reciprocate, to offer in return for what one receives. . . . I become a person by knowing the meaning of receiving and giving. I become a person when I begin to reciprocate" in the "fullness of being in fellowship, and care for others. . . . Indeed, man alone is motivated by the awareness of the insufficiency of sheer being, of sheer living. Man alone is open to the problem of how to be and how not to be at all levels of his existence."[17]

Hasidic scholar Martin Buber puts it this way: We tend to see each person as an "It" or a "Thou." Our "I-It" relationships are based on using other people for our own ends. Our "I-Thou" relationships treat others as God's image bearers worthy of being served and loved.[18] In an I-Thou relationship, we see the other person as a "thou," a gift from God to be appreciated and respected.

At the deepest level, interpersonal conflicts have to do with attitudes and resulting actions, with how we view and correspondingly treat one another. They are about what we do or don't see as our roles and responsibilities in relationships. Are we involved in interpersonal relationships for the sake of ourselves? For other persons? For relationships? For God? These aren't just philosophical questions. They're deeply theological, even biblical ones. And our answers to them have significant, practical consequences for our relationships. They will shape our communicative ideals and how we address the inevitable conflicts. They will determine whether we are satisfied just trying to manage interpersonal conflicts or whether we seek to flourish in community with others.

Like the Old Testament writers, especially the prophets, Heschel and Buber direct us to communicate faithfully for *shalom*—harmonious relations with God, others, and ourselves. The biblical vision of shalom should shape how we see ourselves and others, how we practice everyday interpersonal communication, and how we address conflicts. Shalom reminds us that the deepest joy and delight come not through merely human relationships, not even through conflict-free relationships, but through God-blessed relationships. For Christians, shalom is the kind of relational life in Jesus Christ that nurtures our other two major relationships—with neighbors and with ourselves.

Shalom is biblical life, rich with community and hope, rather than just the absence of negative conflicts. Shalom is the vision of the new heaven and the new earth, the new Jerusalem ("shalom" is one of the root words for "Jeru-*shalom*"). Eugene Peterson says that shalom is "one of the richest words in the Bible." The word "gathers all aspects of wholeness that result from God's will completed in us. Shalom is the work of God that, when complete, releases streams of living water in us and pulsates with eternal life."[19] Shalom is relational life.

We yearn to experience such life. We desire to love and be loved. Deep down, we want to be affirmed in loving relationships. We imagine living joyfully with God, neighbor, and self—without verbal abuse, dishonesty, unfaithfulness, and other relationship-killing communication. We long to be emotionally close and at peace with those we care about and with those who care about us, especially friends, family, and fellow believers. Our best moments as humans, says writer Frederick Buechner, are when "it is possible to escape the squirrel-cage of being me into the landscape of being us."[20] A person does not need to be a superman or superwoman to flourish. An individual flourishes when he or she is "truly living rather than merely existing."[21]

The problem with practicing only "conflict management" in our relationships is that it sets our sights too low. Conflict can destroy relationships over time. But what's the biblical alternative? Not conflict-free communication but, instead, relationships of joy and delight in which conflict is addressed openly, respectfully, and compassionately. Isn't this the type of relationship that we love to dwell in precisely because we all are beloved amid our differences?

Seeking Peace-Filled Relationships

How can we judge the "rightness" or "wrongness" of our person-to-person communication? What relational life-or-death norms should we use to assess our interactions with others?

One set of biblical norms for evaluating communication in terms of shalom has to do with *justice* and *peace*. Shalom offers a rich biblical tradition of emphasizing these two concepts to discern whether relationships are fostering life or death. As Bruce Birch puts it in *To Love as We Are Loved*, "Peace, justice, well-being, wholeness, health, righteousness: all of these things participate in the vision of the reality of shalom."[22]

Shalom as Relational Justice

Shalom includes biblical justice. This justice isn't simply legalistic retribution—a life for a life, an eye for an eye, or a lie for a lie.[23] Jesus says during the Sermon on the Mount, "You have heard that it was said, 'Eye for eye, and tooth for tooth.' But I tell you, do not resist an evil person. If someone slaps you on the right cheek, turn to them the other cheek also."[24]

Biblical justice doesn't give us the right to respond in kind to others' deceptive or abusive communication. No self-serving revenge. No treating others as a thing—an "It." We're called to "incarnate Jesus, the Reconciler and Redeemer."[25] We work as servants of Jesus Christ, not as self-serving manipulators or deceivers. Our "yes" is "yes" and our "no" is "no." Why? Because others deserve truth and respect from us.

Justice is all about giving others what they rightly are due as God's image bearers and our neighbors. They deserve to hear the truth, to be able to participate in communication about their lives and futures, and to be respected even when disagreed with. In short, we all merit both a "say" and an "audience." When we fail to listen to others we treat them as nonexistent. We prejudge—and act with prejudice toward—them.

Shalom as Relational Peace

Biblical peace is not just the lack of conflict and strife but positive relationships for flourishing together. Think of a peaceful setting on the beach with a close friend during a vacation. The rolling waves and light breeze still your souls as you both delight in the place and the companionship. You smile at each other, speechless. Then you say to yourself, "This is the life." This type of *peace*, which Scripture often refers to as *unity*,[26] is marked by the "presence of genuine harmony, understanding, and goodwill between people" and involves a sense of wholeness, contentment, tranquility, and security.[27]

In biblical peace, the wolf will not merely stop attacking the lamb, and the lamb will not only avoid the wolf's territory. The wolf and lamb will feed and live together.[28] That's a tall metaphor for imperfect human beings, but it's also a richly relational metaphor. It's God's plan for life-giving relationships; we are commanded to live at peace with one another,[29] just as Jesus Christ gives us his peace. Attorney Ken Sande, who specializes in biblical peacemaking, writes, "Nothing reveals God's concern for peace more vividly than his decision to send his beloved Son to 'guide our feet into the path of peace.'"[30] As the writer of Proverbs says, when our ways are pleasing to the Lord, we make even our enemies live in peace with us.[31]

In biblical peace, we enjoy our relationships even if we don't always appreciate every aspect of them. College roommates might not suffer from nasty conflicts. But do they experience joy and delight together? Are they in a living rather than dying relationship? Are they respecting each other as God's image bearers? Are they seeking the best for each other?

Faithfulness is the overarching norm for assessing our communication for shalom. In such communication, people are rightly faithful to one another, to God, and to themselves. The goal of faithful interpersonal communication is not just reducing conflict but building relationships filled with justice and peace so that each of us may flourish with God, others, and ourselves.

This book often substitutes the idea of "flourishing" for the biblical word "shalom." It uses the concept of flourishing to encompass personal and communal well-being. *Flourishing* suggests growing, blossoming, and thriving in harmony with others. It's a fitting term for evaluating how well a living thing is doing within its environment.[32] Relationships live and die; they are never static. If we don't feed relationships, they wither and sometimes perish. "I am like an olive tree flourishing in the house of God," writes the psalmist. "I trust in God's unfailing love for ever and ever. For what you have done I will always praise you in the presence of your faithful people. And I will hope in your name, for your name is good."[33]

Kenneth Burke, one of the twentieth century's most influential rhetorical critics, says, "A way of life is an acting-together; and in acting-together, men have common sensations, concepts, images, ideas, attitudes that make them consubstantial."[34] The church father Tertullian (ca. 160–ca. 220) coined the term "consubstantial" ("of one substance") to capture both the oneness of the Trinity and Jesus's spiritual oneness with his followers. Echoing Tertullian, Burke tried to describe some of the mystery of human community using age-old theological terms. We all have a sense that there is more to interpersonal relationships than what we are already experiencing; our deeper desire for community points to shalom, a taste of heaven on earth.

Being Virtuous People

Shalom is a quality of relationships that requires not just communication skills but also people's good character, or *virtue*. The needed virtues include several characteristics.

Being Humble, Not Arrogant

In shalom, we think of others as better than ourselves. We listen and learn. We don't assume we're correct and others are wrong. We question ourselves—including our mixed motives. We're careful about not attributing motives or meaning to others' actions until we've heard from them directly. Even when confronting someone whom we think has wronged us, we go forward with a heart of humility and service.[35]

Humble communicators accept the fact that everyone has tensions in their lives. We all have mixed feelings about many things and are not always sure how to proceed relationally. We acknowledge the strains in our own hearts as well as in our interpersonal relationships.[36] We give up any sense of superiority and do what's right for the relationship. It takes two to begin a friendship, but it takes only one to end a quarrel.[37] We don't have to prove ourselves worthy to others. We live with the kind of humility that makes us free to be our imperfect selves.[38]

FOUR STEPS TO RESOLVING CONFLICT

1. Glorify God: trust, obey, and imitate God in the midst of conflict.
2. Get the log out of your own eye: identify and take responsibility for the ways you've wronged another person.
3. Gently restore: talk with the offender privately and lovingly about the situation.
4. Go and be reconciled: grant forgiveness and pursue genuine reconciliation with the offender.

Adapted from Ken Sande, *The Peacemaker: A Biblical Guide to Resolving Personal Conflict*, 3rd ed. (Grand Rapids: Baker Books, 2004), 12–13.

Being Mild-Mannered, Not Inflammatory

We speak and write with restraint, not with unbridled emotions. Recognizing that how we communicate is just as important as the actual words we use, we calm our souls even in the midst of emotionally charged conflicts. We avoid escalating conflicts. We're temperate and measured, even when our own emotions start boiling. We practice self-control. Even when we've been wronged, we practice healthy rather than combative resistance.[39] "Hate is for emergencies, like a fast battery charge; it is a quick fix like heroin," writes Christian author and ethicist Lewis Smedes. "As a long-term energizer, it is unreliable. And in the end it kills."[40]

Being Gentle, Not Harsh

Our verbal and nonverbal communication is soft and gentle, not angry and brash. We think of our speech as a light breeze rather than a mighty hurricane. A gentle response to someone turns away wrath, but a harsh reply stirs up anger, says the writer of Proverbs.[41] Blessed are the meek—the gentle.[42] Harsh words rub salt into wounds.[43] We speak with grace to those who hear us.[44]

Being Inviting, Not Threatening

We convey a sense of being open to and interested in others. We avoid being the kinds of people who frighten or intimidate others. We're personally hospitable in our hearts and minds. We win people over by first empathizing with them and then communicating *with* them, not *at* them.

Being Cooperative, Not Confrontational

Peaceful communicators seek common ground for conversation, not arguments to win. We're interested in working with others rather than demanding that they agree with us. We welcome collaboration. We're open to win-win compromises. Peaceful communication avoids warlike rhetoric about battles and enemies. This isn't easy because popular culture fosters a warlike atmosphere with winners and losers.

"When was the last time you went to see a movie about peace?" asks theologian Stanley Hauerwas. "War has seized our imagination."[45]

Being Patient, Not Hasty

Communicating for shalom, we accept the long view of nurturing our relationships rather than the short view of quickly resolving all of our conflicts and eliminating all misunderstanding. A fool is hot-headed and reckless, says Proverbs.[46] We admit that communication is complex and needs sensitive, thoughtful consideration. Nuances are important. Getting to know each other takes time. We're patiently on guard against quickly stereotyping others. We accept others' need for time too. We're generous with our time when our neighbor says, "I need time to think about it" or "I can't discuss it right now." As long as two persons keep talking, they are not totally hostile.[47]

Embracing Differences

Shalom embraces differences as well as unity. Biblical peace is a special kind of harmony that fosters delight in the different ways that each person can contribute to the good of a relationship. In today's world, such differences are sometimes limited to obvious distinctions such as ethnicity, gender, disability, and race. Age is important too; young people and senior citizens need to be respected and included in many conversations. We all benefit from the energy of youth and the wisdom of age.

But beyond such relatively obvious distinctions is the more mysterious way that God can use various personalities and cultures to bless relationships. Often those who already hold organizational power need insights from outsiders, especially those on the fringes of society. Many churches don't grow because the members fail to befriend those who are not like existing members and whose communication styles seem so different and even threatening.[48]

The problem is that we're all more comfortable being surrounded with people who are like us. We aim to avoid potential conflicts by maintaining the status quo. The resulting peace is superficially based on an in-group sense of superiority. Moreover, it survives by groups failing to listen to other groups.

Rich relationships don't result from social uniformity because there aren't enough challenges to overcome. Differences of opinion and perspective, when addressed with virtue, can enrich relationships. Artificial peace is marked by people who look, think, and communicate alike, without questioning themselves. Such insincere peace also exists when people don't care enough about their differences to identify and value them. By contrast, real biblical peace is evident when people see and accept their differences as part of the shared blessing of God's richly textured creation and humans' individual and cultural variety.

Every society—and nearly every organization, from churches to workplaces—maintains superficial peace by excluding those who make the members feel uncomfortable. For years this was especially true for predominantly white American groups, which invited few African Americans to participate. This continues to be true for many North American churches, resulting in Sunday being one of the most

CULTURAL DIFFERENCES ABOUT DISAGREEMENT

German Culture	New Zealand, British, Mainland Chinese Culture
Disagreement does not need to be avoided.	Disagreement is to be avoided.
A heated debate is enjoyable and a lack of disagreement is boring.	Seek agreement and common ground.
Disagreement is expressed openly or exacerbated.	Disagreement should be played down.
Emotions are displayed openly.	Emotions are restrained.
Disagreement does not necessarily indicate conflict.	Disagreement is a precursor to conflict.

Adapted from Stefanie Stadler, "Cultural Differences in the Orientation to Disagreement and Conflict," *China Media Research* 9, no. 4 (Fall 2013): 66–75.

segregated days of the week. Imagine how much richer the music alone is in churches that are open to cultural differences. African American spirituals, for instance, carry a wonderful legacy of deeply Christian experience. Such cultural diversity in churches nearly always emerges through the interpersonal relationships of individuals from different traditions.

Human differences represent communicative and cultural capacity because individuals and groups have their own stories that contribute to the mosaic of what it means to be human. For Christians, these stories are also parables that reflect God's grace in the midst of human brokenness. This is partly why it is so critically important for Christians to practice *hospitality*—making room in our hearts, minds, and homes for the "stranger" among us—with those whose stories expand believers' visions of the kingdom of God.

The apostle Paul broke down many existing cultural barriers by proclaiming the gospel to all people—Jew and Greek, male and female, slave and free.[49] He said that all humans can be "one in Christ Jesus" regardless of their individual, cultural, and genetic differences. Paul didn't mean that all cultural practices are good for people's flourishing in Christ and in Christian community; followers of Jesus need wisdom and discernment about culture. But the Christian faith is meant to radically embrace diversity within unity. The oneness in Christ overshadows most of the cultural differences that we use to uphold our own cultural stereotypes and arrogance. Entering into interpersonal relationships with such narrow-minded assumptions about those who are different from us is a recipe for either indifference toward others or peace-robbing conflicts.

Conclusion

Conflicts are inevitable. Some are deeply destructive, seemingly unresolvable. Relationships break down, escalate, and too often simply dissolve. That's what happened to Nancy and David's marriage, leaving them watching television at opposite ends of the house.

But true peace isn't about keeping a lid on conflict and avoiding differences of opinion and culture. Even emotionally intense conflicts are opportunities to grow together by respecting differences and seeking shared goodness. Biblical flourishing is where peace and justice come together as a taste of the new heaven and the new earth—a signpost for all to witness. When we listen as virtuous persons across our differences, we grow to respect one another and to appreciate God's grace.

Following Jesus is a call to be peacemakers by how we live as well as what we say. Our lives speak to others what Jesus's peace truly means to us. Our relationships even affect the integrity of the gospel because life and witness cannot be separated.[50] One of our everyday communicative tasks is to discern what it means to communicate with the kind of peace that passes human understanding as a foretaste of flourishing in eternal life.

As we show in the next chapter, sometimes the only way back to peace is via forgiveness. In fact, forgiveness mirrors what God has done for all repentant sinners through Jesus Christ. Forgiveness allows all of us to restore relationships rather than simply give up on them or let them languish.

8

. . . .
. . . .

RESTORE RELATIONSHIPS

Dear Brian,

I need to apologize to you for some big mistakes I made in my fathering. I hope this [letter] allows us to feel closer to one another. My greatest hope would be for you to forgive me. . . .

I love you.

Dad

This father's apology to his twenty-four-year-old son was long overdue. The father had been physically abusive for years.

The son responded:

Dad,

Thanks for your letter. I have to admit it came as a total surprise, even a shock. . . .

I can begin to forgive you now. . . .

I love you too, Dad. Thanks for writing.

Brian[1]

Both notes were tentative about the future. The son was understandably skeptical about his father's written apology. One brief note can't automatically undo years of hurt and humiliation. But the son concluded with a ray of hope, an expression of love for his abuser.

We don't know if their relationship will ever flourish. But a seed has been planted in new relational soil. We can pray for the father and son as they embark on a journey of healing. May they begin to experience some peace even as shalom seems like a distant dream.

Because we live amid broken relationships, we all have stories of offense and forgiveness.[2] Perhaps we need to seek forgiveness for our own cruel or disrespectful actions. Possibly our unkind words, rolled eyes, or harsh glances hurt a friend. Perhaps we neglected to communicate with a family member or betrayed a spouse. Maybe we cheated on an exam or gossiped about a coworker. Possibly we're wrestling with forgiving ourselves. Maybe we can't see beyond our pain to even imagine forgiving someone whose words deeply hurt us. We all need the transforming gift of forgiveness. "To err is human, to forgive divine," writes Alexander Pope.[3]

As we explain in this chapter, we're called to use the gift of communication responsibly to grant and accept real forgiveness. Such forgiveness is considerably more than tolerance, exoneration, excuses, and even reconciliation.[4] True forgiveness is all about forgiving others as God has forgiven us. Forgiveness is a process of giving up both our hurt and our desire to get back at others. We're most apt to practice forgiveness when we live repentantly, aware of our own transgressions against God and others. Along the way we need to forgive ourselves too. Forgiveness restores some of the brokenness that keeps us from experiencing greater shalom. Every act of forgiveness restores our relationships with God, neighbor, and self.

Granting Forgiveness

New Testament Greek includes two words for "forgive." *Aphiemi* means letting go or releasing. *Charizomai* means bestowing favor freely or unconditionally.[5] The two words capture *forgiveness* as the process of giving up both our hurt and our desire to get back at others.

To grant forgiveness to someone is to communicate from our heart as if the offender never acted improperly. We release the wounding actions to the God of mercy and justice. After all, who are we to cast the first stone at others for their misdeeds? C. S. Lewis writes, "To be a Christian means to forgive the inexcusable because God has forgiven the inexcusable in you."[6]

Such forgiveness can be challenging, even seemingly impossible. When someone deeply hurts us, we generally want revenge. Suppose a friend posts nasty gossip about us online. We respond with hurt, followed by anger, and then maybe even retaliation. We feel the need to get even. In the opening story of this chapter, the son is understandably skeptical of the father's desire to be forgiven. And it would be natural for Brian to be angry and perhaps even to vengefully want his father to pay for the years of abuse.

Biblically speaking, granting forgiveness is the right choice. We don't choose to be hurt or offended; such feelings can overcome us before we have a chance to think about our predicament. But ultimately we decide how to respond. Our responsibility includes how and when we respond—or if we simply let the offense go in silence.

By first listening to God, we remember that we should act like merciful saints, not vindictive sinners. Jesus Christ has forgiven us for the many ways we have mistreated others and thereby hurt God. We acknowledge, accept, and appreciate God's great forgiveness. We are called to "go and do likewise"—to speak forgiveness in the appropriate medium.[7] We choose by grace to replace some of our gut-wrenching anger with compassion, generosity, and even love toward the wrongdoer.[8] And we keep on forgiving—seventy times seventy.[9] In other words, we imitate God's spacious forgiveness rather than pretend to be our own godlike judges and juries.

How can we practice such forgiveness when our hearts are deeply hurting and we want revenge? We can't do it on our own. We can only imitate Jesus's mercy toward us.[10] It's up to us to offer forgiveness even when we know we can't fully forgive without God's grace through the work of the Holy Spirit. We're called to begin the process of forgiveness, which the Spirit will make real. Theologian Fraser Watts says, "We trivialize forgiveness if we see it as only something that we have the capacity to dispense to others, and do not realise that it is also something bigger than ourselves in which we can participate."[11] All forgiveness is a God thing.

Forgiving Others as God Forgives Us

"Dumbledore says people find it far easier to forgive others for being wrong than being right," remarks the character Hermione Granger in J. K. Rowling's *Harry Potter and the Half-Blood Prince*.[12] Real forgiveness is generous, not stingy. It has no strings attached. There's no place for a phrase like, "I promise to forgive you if you promise to never do it again." There are no "ifs" or "buts" in such relationship-restoring pardons. God doesn't say to us, "Hey, shape up by going to church more often, or I won't ever pardon your sins."

Our forgiving is God's grace in action. After all, we know that we're serial offenders. We can promise not to criticize, insult, or embarrass others, but can we follow through? A father asks forgiveness and promises never again to criticize his seemingly overweight daughter. Will he keep that promise? What if he slips again even as he tries hard to love his daughter unconditionally? We always need to ask and receive forgiveness humbly, seeing ourselves as well as others in need of God's help. True forgiveness involves both grace and mercy for everyone involved.[13] Such forgiveness is a God-blessed way of life, a daily attitude, a compassionate heart that colors our view of others and ourselves.

When we offer forgiveness, we imitate Jesus and model how we would like to be treated. When we grant a pardon, we mercifully refuse to punish the one who deserves it. When a friend breaks his or her promise to keep something about us confidential, we realize that we've done it to others too. We're like the offending friend. We both need kindness in the face of our own relationship-robbing communication. We need to treat others the way we would want—and need—to be treated.

It's a very tall order for us to genuinely say "I forgive you," because it tells the offender that we won't dwell on the hurtful incident. It says that we won't use the incident against the person—and that we don't want the offense to keep us from restoring our relationship.[14]

FOUR PROMISES OF FORGIVENESS

1. "I will not dwell on the hurtful actions."
2. "I will not use the incident to bring you harm."
3. "I will not gossip about it."
4. "I will not allow the incident to keep us from restoring our relationship."

Adapted from Ken Sande, *The Peacemaker: A Biblical Guide to Resolving Personal Conflict*, 3rd ed. (Grand Rapids: Baker Books, 2004), 209.

It says that we're going to cease any gossip about the misdeed and wish the other person well, including in front of others. It says that we're going to advance the person's good name even if the incident harmed our reputation. It can even say that we're going to seek God's blessing on that person.[15] Ethicist Lewis B. Smedes writes, "You will know that forgiveness has begun when you recall those who hurt you and feel the power to wish them well."[16]

Avoiding Common Misunderstandings

There are at least five common misunderstandings of forgiveness.

Forgiving isn't a form of forgetting.

The saying "forgive and forget" isn't quite right. Forgetting isn't the ultimate test of forgiveness. The real test is to treat the person as if the offense had never happened[17] and to embrace the gradual healing of pain.[18] In fact, remembering can help ensure that the offense doesn't recur and allows us to use healing memories to minister to those who are hurting.[19] Our recollections can help us to avoid repeatedly making the same mistakes—both hurting others and failing to pardon them. "Forgiveness is not about forgetting," says Papa, the character who represents God the Father in the best-selling Christian novel *The Shack*. "It is about letting go of another person's throat."[20]

Forgiving isn't just excusing the offense.

Asking for forgiveness isn't about explaining or rationalizing how we've misused the gift of communication at someone else's expense. Forgiveness isn't about listening to and accepting others' excuses for why they hurt us. If they intended to hurt us, we can't simply accept their excuse—as if they didn't mean to hurt us. Offenders can play fast and loose with excuses without ever really admitting their offenses and changing their future actions. Excuses cheapen forgiveness. The greatest sign of hope in Brian's relationship with his father is that his father seeks forgiveness. If Brian simply excused his father regardless of his father's attitude, there might be little chance for long-term healing.

Some transgressions are far too intentional to allow simple excuses. For instance, there's no excuse for spreading dirty little rumors, for verbally humiliating people in front of others, or for destroying a child's self-esteem by incessantly belittling him or her. Likewise, there's no excuse for failing to speak up to defend a friend who is being wrongly charged with misconduct. In such situations we shouldn't merely shrug off the wrongdoing, close our eyes to the seriousness of it, and accept excuses. The situations call for justice as well as peace.

Renee struggled to forgive the hospital staff that, despite her protests that her husband wasn't ready to be discharged, sent him home while he was still suffering from a severe psychological disorder. Shortly after his discharge, he took his own life, leaving Renee to raise their two young daughters. "It's probably one of the hardest things I've ever had to do. Every fiber of my natural being resists it," but if "I am to walk in obedience to God, I must forgive those who have sinned against me," Renee concluded.[21] The hospital's actions were probably inexcusable, but for Renee they were ultimately forgivable.

We need to consider the real depth and impact of specific communicative hurts. On the one hand, is forgiveness really needed, or is the incident relatively trivial? On the other hand, is forgiveness inadequate? A tiny fib is a minor thing; repeated character assassination is far more damaging. For instance, a verbal abuser needs to be held accountable. It won't serve the abuser or the victims if we forget, deny, overlook, or trivialize the wrongdoing.

Forgiving isn't tolerating.

When communication is horribly wrong, none of us should simply have to live with it. We can accept the fact that people forget to offer thanks to others or occasionally lose their tempers and say or write words they soon regret. But we ought not to tolerate being verbally or nonverbally bullied in person or via social media. And we ought not to let others suffer such emotional trauma either. God doesn't call us to remain victims but instead to courageously face and lovingly address the injustice.[22]

Forgiving isn't exonerating.

Exoneration requires restitution from the wrongdoer before favor is bestowed; forgiveness does not. For instance, if someone tells lies that damage our reputation, they work toward restoring our reputation before being exonerated. We should seek to forgive them, but we should not tolerate more slander. The person needs to cease the offenses, ask forgiveness, and repair the damage; then we can begin exonerating. Our willingness to forgive, however, is not contingent on the wrongdoer's willingness to offer restitution.

Forgiving isn't complete reconciliation.

Although we forgive others both to glorify God and to restore our relationships, *reconciliation* (restored relationship) often takes longer. In Luke 15, a wayward son squanders his inheritance before returning home, where his father forgives him. In that case, the gracious father (representing God) and the disobedient son (a sinner before God) were immediately reconciled. In real life, the relationship might take months or years to restore. Trust was lost. The father was humiliated. Reconciliation takes time for healing.

An Amish community quickly reached out to the family of a young man who shot and killed five Amish girls at school. Within a day after experiencing such awful pain, the Amish families sent words of hope to the family of the killer. A close friend of the victims shared with the press: "If you have Jesus in your heart and He has forgiven you . . . [how] can you not forgive other people?"[23] Maybe in such an amazing case of forgiveness God had already been at work, forming the community of faith to be ready for reconciliation long before the tragic event.

We might truly forgive someone who has hurt us deeply, but the relationship may never be fully restored.[24] All restoration is a matter of God's grace, not human devices. We begin the process with God's help. "Forgiveness is a work of God's love in the human soul that compels one to give oneself for another, despite being sinned against, so that the other might love God more deeply," write psychologists Robert Cheong and Frederick DiBlasio.[25] But accepting the fact that someone may never wish to seek a fuller reconciliation with us is one of the most difficult emotional trials in life.

Living in Mutual Forgiveness

Forgiveness is a mutual way of life that makes reconciliation possible. Repentant persons employ the gift of communication repeatedly to breathe new life into fractured relationships. They know that people will offend one another, but they continually nurture a contrite spirit and seek to be more forgiving with each other. They value living in a forgiving community of friends and family.

The Greek word for "repent" is *metanoia*—to change one's understanding.[26] When we forgive, we are actually changing our minds about blame and revenge. We realize that what occurred was wrong

---

SIX SIGNS WE'RE NOT SERIOUS ABOUT FORGIVING OTHERS

1. Stewing about reasons not to forgive
2. Seeking revenge
3. Demanding justice
4. Withholding trust
5. Avoiding the whole incident
6. Complaining that forgiveness is too much work

but also that there might be more to the story that leads to mutual forgiveness. We have to alter our understanding of (1) how we offend one another through communicative action, (2) the extent of our sins, and (3) the greater story of God's mercy. In other words, friends who forgive are living out the gospel in their relationships.

Repentance requires that we candidly confess our sin. To put it differently, we need to speak the truth about ourselves to ourselves

---

REACH: Steps to Forgiveness

- Recall the hurt
- Empathize with the wrongdoer
- Altruistically offer forgiveness
- Commit publicly to forgive
- Hold on to forgiveness

Adapted from Everett L. Worthington, *Forgiving and Reconciling: Bridges to Wholeness and Hope* (Downers Grove, IL: InterVarsity, 2003), 73–74.

---

and before the face of God. Such frank, self-indicting truthtelling reunites us with God and begins releasing the power of forgiveness.[27]

After repentance, we face the hardest part. We have to courageously ask God and then neighbor for the forgiveness that we don't deserve. There's no way around it. We could just try to treat the other person kindly in the future and hope that he or she gets the message that we're sorry for what we've done. That way we wouldn't have to risk rejection. Although it's a good start, and sometimes that's all we can handle emotionally, we need to ask the one we've hurt for forgiveness.

Of course, how we ask for forgiveness is critically important. We need to directly admit our actions. Forgiveness is more likely to occur when we offer a genuine apology that indicates remorse, acknowledges the severity of the offense, and promises better actions in the future.[28] We need to listen to the offended express their emotions—the hurt, the anger, the embarrassment, and perhaps even the outrage. And we need to acknowledge and accept their emotions.[29] The person we offended should be able to see in our faces that we are truly repentant and genuinely seek their forgiveness.[30] A contrite face speaks volumes.

After asking for forgiveness, we need to patiently allow the one we offended adequate time to consider the request and to work through the hurt. Forcing an immediate response is disrespectful.

We also need to turn away from our own patterns of destructive actions. If we mistreated one person in a particular way, chances are we mistreat others similarly. For instance, we all know people who tend to deceive, flatter, or criticize. So when we pledge to the person we offended never to do wrong to them again, we have to realize that we might be making a very significant promise that goes against our tendencies.

If our offense is one of our common weaknesses, we need to do more than just pledge never to do it again to that particular person. Our plan should consist of specific steps, including a system of accountability, that will move us toward stopping the offensive action.[31] We might have to pledge to stop the hurtful actions and specify how we intend to live out the commitment under the watchful eyes and ears of trusted friends.

Perhaps nothing better prepares us to forgive others than our own regular acts of confession before the face of God. By confessing to God our communicative sins of omission and commission, we'll be much better equipped to accept others' weaknesses and forgive them accordingly. Confession humbles us and makes us more virtuous communicators.

Forgiving Ourselves

"I'll never be able to forgive myself." Really? Why?

For some of us, self-loathing is tangible. We carry a lot of guilt and self-criticism. We find it easier to forgive people who have treated us poorly than to forgive ourselves for our own, less grievous offenses. We can end up being so principled that we never buckle under the weight of our own humanity.[32]

We all know that our interpersonal communication regularly falls short. We replay past conversations in our minds, thinking about what we could have said or how we could have acted differently. Maybe we could have been more patient, listening better before speaking or writing. Religious and nonreligious individuals alike express difficulty in forgiving themselves, despite the fact that religious individuals are more likely to forgive others, to feel forgiven by God, and to seek forgiveness.[33]

Jesus doesn't call us to love others without loving ourselves. Instead of getting down on ourselves, we are called to forgive ourselves as we forgive our neighbors. Holding grudges against ourselves is no better than holding them against others. Biblically speaking, friends forgive. We are friends of Jesus, who forgives us, and friends with ourselves. To be a self-forgiving friend is a marvelous gift from and to God.

Conclusion

Brian's abusive father sent his son a note requesting forgiveness. Presumably he wanted to reconnect with his son. Brian's open response, in turn, suggested that father and son might be able to meet in the grace of slow but steady healing. There were no guarantees. Wrongs had been committed. Brian had legitimate concerns. Was his father simply trying to make himself feel better, or was he genuinely repentant?

For believers, forgiveness is a way of accepting and demonstrating the love of Christ to the world. We gratefully forgive others and ourselves because God has unconditionally forgiven us through the blood of Jesus Christ. Every act of forgiveness is an opportunity to develop a more intimate relationship with God, neighbor, and self.

In the concluding chapter we celebrate the miracle of interpersonal relationships and call for a balance between traditional and newer ways of communicating. Social media hold great promise for building friendships, but so do older means of interaction, which we need to nurture or else risk losing. The joy of relationships is more limited by our everyday routines than by the available forms of communication.

CONCLUSION

Celebrate Friendships

The great Christian author C. S. Lewis wrote, "Friendship is the greatest of worldly goods. Certainly to me it is the chief happiness of life." He added that if he had to give advice to a young person about where to live, he would recommend this: "Sacrifice almost everything to live where you can be near your friends."[1]

Could friendship really be the greatest pleasure in life? Do we have to dwell by our friends to truly enjoy them?

Lewis wrote before email, social media, and live video calls. He was an avid letter writer and a conversationalist with friends—especially at the local pub. But how would he have conducted his life today, when long-distance calls are free, many writers blog, and publishers like to send popular writers on book promotion tours?

This concluding chapter, inspired by Lewis's remarkable writings on friendship and love, is a call to nurture and celebrate friendship through all of the media at our disposal. It's also a chapter about using insights from previous chapters to discern specifically how to form great friendships in the age of social media. Many of the points in this chapter expand upon and integrate communicative practices addressed in previous chapters.

In the first section of the chapter, we focus on the joy of being an intentional builder of life-affirming friends rather than just a tagalong friend amid life's distractions. Next, we consider the benefits of "mini-Sabbaths" as means for growing deeper in self-knowledge and relational wisdom. In the subsequent section we show that some of the best relational activities are simple, low-stress, fun times together that foster openness. Then we look at selecting the right medium for the right friendships at the right time. Finally, we return to the theme of chapter 1: gratitude. If C. S. Lewis is right about friendship being "the chief happiness of life" on earth, we all have much to celebrate in every friend. If we accept that friendship is a gracious gift, we can both give and receive it—by being a friend and by having friends—as a cherished offering.

Being Intentional

If you want a friend, be a friend. That sounds simple. Is it?

Yes and no. We do have to reach out in friendship if we want to have friends. But some potential friends might not reciprocate. Others might suffocate us with so much attention that we can't attend to other relationships.

Friendship is inherently mutual. It takes two willing and able participants. If you want to befriend, you have to become a genuine friend. You have to help get the mutuality rolling.

Thanks to the way God created us as communicative beings, we can be intentional about friendship. We can listen and pay attention to what others are saying and doing. And within that pool of people we can put our sights on those with whom we seem to resonate. They appear to laugh at similar things. Their faces seem inviting. They make us want to be around them, hear their stories, and tell ours.

When such friendship seems possible, what do we do? For one thing, it's easy to get scared off. What if the other person rejects us? Do we have enough courage? Do we need a lot of encouragement? "To love at all is to be vulnerable," writes C. S. Lewis in *The Four Loves*.[2] For another thing, we can be too busy and miss the opportunity to build a relationship. The clutter of media messages is especially vexing. We want to stay connected with other, even more distant acquaintances. Social media tug us in all kinds of directions.

For many of us it's just too easy to become a kind of tagalong acquaintance of many others, pretending that we have a lot of friends when we might not have even a handful of the kinds of biblical friends that are mutually enjoyable and self-sacrificing. We just can't seem to get relational traction. Perhaps we lack intentionality more than communication skills.

C. S. Lewis wrote many great articles and books. He was truly prolific. But he was also available and willing to befriend others, both locally and through correspondence. He met his eventual wife via letters—decades before online dating. And he maintained friendships with nearby literary people like J. R. R. Tolkien, Owen Barfield, and Charles Williams; they called themselves "The Inklings." Reading each other's manuscripts was the academic excuse for meeting. Delight might have been the principal reason.

God can give us friendships in the most amazingly unplanned ways. Yet God also gives us hearts and minds for reaching out intentionally to possible friends. If you want friends, be an intentional friend.

Taking Mini-Sabbaths

How do we get from identifying possible friends to friendship itself? Of course it takes time together, along with intentionality. But what's at the heart of forming friendships?

A best friend works personally on becoming the kind of person who can be such a fine friend. Actually, becoming a virtuous friend is not simply work. It also requires a type of leisure, a form of Sabbath-keeping. Regular mini-Sabbaths for reflection and growth are the key. When our souls are restful, friendships form all around us. When our souls are restless, we scare off potential friends.

Amid the joy of friendship ought to be leisurely time to be alone and reflect on one's self and one's friends. C. S. Lewis says, "Love is not affectionate feeling, but a steady wish for the loved person's ultimate good as far as it can be obtained."[3] We discover how to love a particular friend by listening to them and to ourselves. We first interact with them in person or via media. Then we think about what they mean to us and why we appreciate them. We also ponder their needs. Do they need our encouragement? Do they need a listener? Someone to chat with about life? Someone to enjoy life with? What kinds of things do they enjoy doing? Do we even know?

Imagine taking half-hour mini-Sabbath excursions all alone, but with friends in your heart and on your mind. You'll discover two things: how best to love your friends and why to give thanks for them in spite of their foibles and quirks. In fact, you'll come to appreciate their quirkiness by releasing excessive control over these relationships. You'll relax and enjoy what God is doing for both you and your friends, and you'll be better prepared to serve your friends as you interact with them.

The gift of metacommunication—communication about communication—is truly wondrous. We can discuss with ourselves how well we are doing as friends of others. We can recall and ponder our experiences. What did we last really enjoy about a particular friend? Would we be willing to share that with the person—maybe in a quick text message or the next time we meet? What are the strains on the friendship? How would we talk with our friend about those strains? Do any of our friendships show the spark of something deeper, perhaps romantic love?

Sometimes such self-reflection can be a bit painful, especially when we consider miscommunication or even intentionally destructive communication that led to misunderstandings and hurts. But if we can't face those difficulties with ourselves on a mini-Sabbath, how can we face them with others? There is a kind of healing pain that comes with being honest with ourselves relationally. C. S. Lewis writes, "Pain insists upon being attended to. God whispers to us in our pleasures, speaks in our consciences, but shouts in our pains. It is his megaphone to rouse a deaf world."[4] We need our pleasures, consciences, and pains to move ahead.

In your mini-Sabbaths, count your friends by name. Thank them for being friends. And thank our greatest Friend for the gift of communication that makes friendship so delightful.

Enjoying Relational Activities

Often communication works oppositely. We try hard and it gets worse. We let go and it gets better. In the case of friendship, too, sometimes not trying so hard is the best route. This is marvelously baffling.

The mystery has to do with the conditions we create for friends and potential friends to be open with us. When we try to force self-disclosure, people often clam up. When self-disclosure comes naturally through conducive circumstances, people are more likely to talk about the most revealing aspects of their lives as well as listen to others.

Whether online or in person, the same rule of self-disclosure applies: warm, hospitable environments lead people to open up, whereas harsh, forced environments shut people down. Comforting situations are the most appealing for forming friendships. Shaming situations are the most suffocating.

So one thing to think about during a mini-Sabbath is the type of activities that are most naturally relational. Sharing meals or snacks together has always stimulated people to tell stories and offer mutual self-disclosure. Another longtime catalyst of friendships, especially within families and extended families, has been vacations. In recent decades the road trip has become the nonfamilial equivalent of mobile friendship formation. Group games, especially those that are not time-constrained, are important contexts for personal revelations and sometimes even fairly serious conversations. In fact, many traditional board games are still enormously popular partly because they offer a means to warm fellowship among friends. Playing the game can be enjoyable itself, but the uninhibited conversation that takes place makes the event much more meaningful.

Beyond planned relational activities are spontaneous situations arising from everyday interaction. We get a last-minute text inviting us to hang out with friends or head out for coffee. Someone invites us to jog or walk with them, to head for the beach or the forest, the trail or the supermarket. God too must take delight in these unpredictable biddings to fellowship. God knows no ordinary bounds to human interactions. All of earth is the Lord's, to be explored, enjoyed, and employed to serve others.

Yet if we're not careful these unplanned opportunities can slip away. They can seem so impractical, even invasive upon our carefully crafted daily schedules. What about friends giving us notice in advance? What about giving us time to think about it? Does the Holy Spirit care about our anxiousness and busyness? Dare we consider the potential value of an unplanned invitation to spend time with another human being?

Selecting Fitting Media

Some theologians call the development of human culture the "opening up" of God's original creation.[5] From this perspective, all of the culture that human beings create expands upon God's initial formation of the earth and beyond. Culture encompasses all technologies, including all communication-related technologies like mass and social media. Once humans created languages millennia ago, they began converting those linguistic symbol systems into stone, parchment, paper, electronic, and eventually digital media. Moreover, digital technologies are usurping earlier paper and electronic media, such as news periodicals, books, and audio and video recordings. We live in a digital multimedia universe increasingly accessed by cell phones.

Where does or should friendship fit into this universe of overlapping means of communication? Because friendship depends on people knowing each other fairly well, the most appropriate media would have enough emotional bandwidth to allow two or more people to listen well and speak openly without excessive visual, textual, or vocal interruptions.

Clearly God's formation of human beings as highly linguistic creatures puts speaking and listening at the forefront of interpersonal technologies. Our tongues and ears are amazing technologies, followed by our bodies in general, including gestures and facial expressions. If we have to pick one medium, then, humans' greatest relational bandwidth is in-person interaction. This is simply how we are made.

Moreover, all five human senses can be involved in in-person interaction. A kiss combines all senses—sight, sound, touch, taste, and smell. Today we equate kissing with sexuality, but this was not so much the case in New Testament times. The "holy kiss" referred to four times in the New Testament was the early church's version of a common greeting.[6] In the Middle East at that time, kisses were used publicly like a handshake is used today, and the church picked up on the practice as a kind of personal peace offering and sign of fellowship. Such kisses are still practiced in some parts of the world, such as Argentina and many Arab nations.

Perhaps today a hug is closer than a handshake to the kind of sign of friendship embodied in the holy kiss. Hugs can be tricky business; men often feel awkward hugging each other, and cross-gender hugging is frowned upon in some circles. Nevertheless, a friendship hug can be a splendid form of communication among friends, regardless of whether they have seen each other recently. A verbal greeting or words of encouragement combined with a hug symbolize friendship and highlight the emotional bandwidth of in-person interaction.

Of course there are all kinds of ways for people to initiate and develop friendships in person and online. If the goal is to develop strong in-person friendships with wide emotional bandwidth, many media can help get friends there. The rise of social media has been a tremendous blessing for many people, including those with disabilities, social anxiety, extreme shyness, and isolated locations. As social media move toward audio and video along with text, their emotional bandwidth increasingly emulates in-person interaction. Although it's difficult to carry on a long-term romantic relationship online, nonromantic friendships are progressively made possible. Just as colleagues can stay in touch with live text, audio, and video while telecommuting, friends online can be digitally present to each other in real time.

One of our goals as Christians in the age of social media should be to discern which media are most appropriate for different stages and types of relationships, including friendship. The question is how we rightly fit together the medium and the message—the *fittingness* of different media with different communicative aspects of friendship. Taken to extremes, the answers seem obvious: Who would propose marriage to another person via texting? Who would seek via email forgiveness for a terrible wrong when the phone would be more personably fitting? What if the parties were not able to get together in person? But what about other friendship-building and friendship-maintaining communicative actions like celebrating, encouraging, promising, and questioning?

All media ultimately are gifts from God to use in fitting ways to love him, our neighbors, and ourselves. We should celebrate our options even as we struggle a bit to know how best to use older and newer media wisely and well.

Giving Thanks

C. S. Lewis writes, "Friendship is unnecessary, like philosophy, like art. . . . It has no survival value; rather it is one of those things which give value to survival."[7] In other words, friendship is a valuable gift that gives our lives meaning. We could live without it, but what would our lives be like? Who could stand the loneliness, the sense that we are lost in our own individual selves without hope for emotionally fulfilling relationships?

Even writing about friendship seems to devalue friendship. In a way, friendship is to be experienced, enjoyed, and celebrated more than it is to be examined, picked apart, and put back together by communication experts or anyone else. Friendship itself is right and fitting for our lives, even one of the tastes of heaven on earth. In true friendship there is considerable shalom.

In an age when there is so much stress about finding one's calling in life, we might do well to think of friendship as one of our greatest callings. We're called by no less than our Redeemer to follow him into the joy of friendship. We're not called solely to careers; we're called to befriend others just as Jesus Christ has befriended us.

Conclusion

Great interpersonal relationships, including friendships, result from a fascinating combination of God's grace and our efforts. If they were just a product of human work, we would all be stressed out. But the Spirit is walking alongside us, piquing our interests in particular people, cautioning us against ignoring or smothering others, inviting us to walk ahead in the knowledge that God wants the best for each one of us. God doesn't wish for us to be alone any more than God himself would want to be alone, without the Trinity.

So as we walk ahead in faith, we attend to the skills and virtues that will equip us for great interpersonal relationships. We are to be grateful, listen attentively, single-task, know ourselves, relate openly, encourage others, promote peace, and restore relationships by offering and granting forgiveness. The result is friendships with God, neighbor, and self that are truly worthy of celebrating.

APPENDIX

Using *An Essential Guide to Interpersonal Communication* as a Supplemental Textbook

The chart below provides suggestions for aligning chapters from *An Essential Guide to Interpersonal Communication* with common chapter titles and topics in major interpersonal communication textbooks. Prospective users of this book are also encouraged to contact the authors.

An Essential Guide to Interpersonal Communication	Mainstream Interpersonal Communication Textbooks
Chapter 1: Be Grateful	Introduction; competence; community
Chapter 2: Listen Attentively	Listening; empathy
Chapter 3: Single-Task	Perceiving others; technology
Chapter 4: Know Yourself	Self construct; managing identities
Chapter 5: Relate Openly	Self-disclosure; expressing emotions
Chapter 6: Encourage Others	Verbal and nonverbal communication; confirming messages
Chapter 7: Promote Peace	Conflict; power; gender; culture
Chapter 8: Restore Relationships	Forgiveness
Conclusion: Celebrate Friendships	Types of relationships

Notes

Chapter 1 Be Grateful

1. "Everything's Amazing and Nobody's Happy," Conan O'Brien Show, You-Tube video, 4:12, posted by Matt Bedard, January 4, 2014, https://www.youtube.com/watch?v=uEY58fiSK8E.

2. James M. Houston, *The Heart's Desire: Satisfying the Hunger of the Soul* (Colorado Springs: NavPress, 1996), 25.

3. Thomas á Kempis, *The Imitation of Christ*, trans. Joseph N. Tylenda (New York: Random House, 1998), 83.

4. Ibid., 5.

5. John Baillie, *The Sense of the Presence of God* (Oxford: Oxford University Press, 1962), 237.

6. Exod. 15–17.

7. David W. Pao, *Thanksgiving: An Investigation of a Pauline Theme* (Downers Grove, IL: InterVarsity, 2002), 145.

8. Ibid., 147.

9. Prov. 3:3.

10. Abraham J. Heschel, *Who Is Man?* (Stanford, CA: Stanford University Press, 1965), 114.

11. Robert Raynolds, *In Praise of Gratitude: An Invitation to Trust in Life* (New York: Harper & Brothers, 1961), 24.

12. Robert Emmons, *Thanks! How the New Science of Gratitude Can Make You Happier* (New York: Houghton Mifflin, 2007), 5.

13. Karl Barth, *Church Dogmatics* 4/1, *Reconciliation*, ed. Geoffrey W. Bromiley and Thomas Forsyth Torrance, trans. Geoffrey W. Bromiley (London: T&T Clark, 1956), 42, quoted in Eugene Peterson, *A Long Obedience in the Same Direction: Discipleship in an Instant Society* (Downers Grove, IL: InterVarsity, 2000), 198.

14. 1 Thess. 5:16–18.

15. Alvin Plantinga, *Warranted Christian Belief* (New York: Oxford University Press, 2000), 293.

16. Michael E. McCullough, Robert A. Emmons, and Jo-Ann Tsang, "The Grateful Disposition: A Conceptual and Empirical Topography," *Journal of Personality and Social Psychology* 82, no. 1 (2002): 112–27.

17. Robert A. Emmons and Teresa T. Kneezel, "Giving Thanks: Spiritual and Religious Correlates of Gratitude," *Journal of Psychology and Christianity* 24, no. 2 (2005): 140–48.

18. Flannery O'Connor, *A Prayer Journal* (New York: Farrar, Straus & Giroux, 2013), 17.

19. Mayo Mathers, "Radical Gratitude: What a Dying Friend Taught Me about Being Thankful 'In All Things,'" *Today's Christian Woman*, November/December 2006, 44.

20. Ibid., 45.

21. John Donne, *The Best of John Donne* (Colorado Springs: Balster, 2012), 46.

22. James W. Carey, *Culture as Communication: Essays on Media and Society* (Boston: Unwin Hyman, 1989), 18.

23. Victoria Taylor, "Woman, 26, Posts Craigslist Ad Asking to Rent Family for the Holiday," *New York Daily News*, December 20, 2013, http://www.nydailynews.com/news/national/woman-craigslist-ad-rent-mom-dad-article-1.1540683.

24. Bill Strom, *The Relationship Project: Moving from "You and Me" to "We"* (Kansas City, MO: Beacon Hill, 2014), 42.

25. Esther de Waal, *Living with Contradiction: An Introduction to Benedictine Spirituality* (Harrisburg, PA: Morehouse), 81.

Chapter 2 Listen Attentively

1. Juanita Westaby, "Episcopalian Monk Compares Prayer Life to Dating Relationship," *Grand Rapids Press*, March 25, 2000, B5.

2. Ernest Hemingway, *By-Line Ernest Hemingway: Selected Articles and Dispatches of Four Decades*, ed. William White (New York: Scribner, 1998), 219.

3. John Shotter, "Listening in a Way That Recognizes the World of 'the Other,'" *The International Journal of Listening* 23, no. 1 (2009): 21.

4. Cari Jackson, *The Gift to Listen, the Courage to Hear* (Minneapolis: Augsburg Fortress, 2003), 2.

5. Sharon Jayson, "Cellphones and Texting Have Blown Up the Dating Culture," *USA Today*, July 19, 2013, http://www.usatoday.com/story/news/nation/2013/07/18/mobile-dating-behavior-technology/2500359/.

6. Winston Churchill, *Churchill by Himself: The Definitive Collection of Quotations*, ed. Richard Langworth (London: Ebury, 2008), 572.

7. Stephen Covey, *The Seven Habits of Highly Effective People* (New York: Simon & Schuster, 1989), 251.

8. Lisbeth Lipari, "Listening Otherwise: The Voice of Ethics," *The International Journal of Listening* 23, no. 1 (2009): 45. See also, Lisbeth Lipari, "Listening, Thinking, Being," *Communication Theory* 20, no. 3 (2010): 348–62.

9. Stephanie Bennett, "Seeking the Sound of Silence: Human Presence and the Acoustics of Solitude," *Proceedings of the Media Ecology Association* 11 (2010): 53–66.

10. Ronald C. Arnett, Leeanne M. Bell, and Janie M. Harden Fritz, "Dialogic Learning as First Principle in Communication Ethics," *Atlantic Journal of Communication* 18, no. 3 (2010): 123.

11. Deut. 30:11–20.

12. See, e.g., Matt. 11:15; Mark 4:9, 23; Luke 14:35.

13. Ellen T. Charry, *By the Renewing of Your Minds: The Pastoral Function in Christian Doctrine* (New York: Oxford University Press, 1999), 3.

14. Tony Campolo and Mary Albert Darling, *Connecting Like Jesus: Practices for Healing, Teaching, and Preaching* (San Francisco: Jossey-Bass, 2010), 12–13.

15. Corey L. M. Keyes and Jonathan Haidt, "Introduction: Human Flourishing—The Study of That Which Makes Life Worthwhile," in *Flourishing: Positive Psychology and the Life Well-Lived*, ed. Corey L. M. Keyes and Jonathan Haidt (Washington, DC: American Psychological Association, 2003), 6.

16. Rick Wise and Barb Wise, "Impacting Lives: Reality, Hope and Commitment," WiseChoices, http://www.wise-choices.org/ourstory.html.

17. Rick Wise and Barb Wise, "About WiseChoices," WiseChoices, http://www.wise-choices.org/about.html.

18. Lipari, "Listening Otherwise," 56.

19. Frederick Buechner, *The Clown in the Belfry: Writings on Faith and Fiction* (New York: HarperCollins, 1992), 97.

20. Mark 12:30–31.

21. Epicurus, *Vatican Sayings* 52, quoted in *The Epicurus Reader: Selected Writings and Testimonia*, trans. and ed. Brad Inwood and Lloyd P. Gerson (Indianapolis: Hackett, 1994), xii.

22. Marsha Dutton, *Aelred of Rievaulx: The Historical Works*, trans. Jane Patricia Freeland (Kalamazoo, MI: Cistercian, 2005), 26.

23. John 15.

24. John 15:12–13.

25. Harper Lee, *To Kill a Mockingbird* (New York: Grand Central, 1988), 39.

26. Gen. 2:18.

27. Gen. 1:26, italics added.

Chapter 3 Single-Task

1. Dave Crenshaw, *The Myth of Multitasking: How "Doing It All" Gets Nothing Done* (San Francisco: Jossey-Bass, 2008); Jim Taylor, "Technology: Myth of Multitasking," *Psychology Today*, March 30, 2011, http://www.psychologytoday.com/blog/the-power-prime/201103/technology-myth-multitasking.

2. Mike Snider, "Survey: Video Gamers More Social and More Socially Conscious," *USA Today*, June 5, 2014, http://www.usatoday.com/story/tech/gaming/2014/06/05/video-game-players-stereotypes-debunked/10008019.

3. Douglas D. Webster, *Soul Craft: How God Shapes Us through Relationships* (Downers Grove, IL: InterVarsity, 1999), 36.

4. Eugene H. Peterson, *Where Your Treasure Is: Psalms That Summon You from Self to Community* (Grand Rapids: Eerdmans, 1985), 153.

5. Charles R. Berger and Richard J. Calabrese, "Some Explorations in Initial Interaction and Beyond: Toward a Developmental Theory of Interpersonal Communication," *Human Communication Research* 1, no. 2 (1975): 99–112.

6. Brennan Manning, *Abba's Child: The Cry of the Heart for Intimate Belonging* (Colorado Springs: NavPress, 2002), 53.

7. "Isolated Americans Trying to Connect," *USA Today*, August 5, 2006, http://usatoday30.usatoday.com/news/nation/2006-08-05-lonely-americans_x.htm.

8. Miller McPherson, Lynn Smith-Lovin, and Matthew E. Brashears, "Social Isolation in America: Changes in Core Discussion Networks over Two Decades," *American Sociological Review* 71, no. 3 (June 2006): 353–75.

9. Young-ok Yum, "The Relationships among Loneliness, Self/Partner Constructive Maintenance Behavior, and Relational Satisfaction in Two Cultures," *Communication Studies* 54, no. 4 (Winter 2003): 451–67.

10. Leslie A. Baxter and Barbara M. Montgomery, *Relating: Dialogues and Dialectics* (New York: Guilford, 1996).

11. Cathy Gulli, "Cut the Digital 'Tether': Stop Texting Mom!," *Maclean's*, November 2, 2013, http://www.macleans.ca/society/technology/stop-texting-mom.

12. Andrew M. Ledbetter, Sarah Heiss, Kenny Sibal, Eimi Lev, Michele Battle-Fisher, and Natalie Shubert, "Parental Invasion and Children's Defensive Behaviors at Home and Away at College: Mediated Communication and Privacy Boundary Management," *Communication Studies* 61, no. 2 (2010): 184–204.

13. Alexandra Sifferlin, "Textual Relations: Couples Who Text Too Much Aren't as in Love as They Want You to Think," *Time*, October 31, 2013, http://healthland.time.com/2013/10/31/if-your-guy-is-texting-you-a-lot-hes-not-that-into-you.

14. Jin Borae and Pena F. Jorge, "Mobile Communication in Romantic Relationships: Mobile Phone Use, Relational Uncertainty, Love, Commitment, and Attachment Styles," *Communication Reports* 23, no. 1 (2010): 39–51.

15. Nancy Baym, Yan Bing Zhang, Adrianne Kunkel, Andrew Ledbetter, and Mei-Chen Lin, "Relational Quality and Media Use in Interpersonal Relationships," *New Media and Society* 9, no. 5 (2007): 735–52.

16. Dmitri Williams, Scott Caplan, and Li Xiong, "Can You Hear Me Now? The Impact of Voice in an Online Gaming Community," *Human Communication Research* 33, no. 4 (2007): 427–49.

17. Rom. 7:18–19.

18. Lloyd John Ogilvie, *Conversation with God: Experiencing the Life-Changing Impact of Personal Prayer* (Eugene, OR: Harvest House), 36.

19. Eccles. 11:4.

20. Neil Lavender and Alan A. Cavaiola, *Impossible to Please: How to Deal with Perfectionistic Coworkers, Controlling Spouses, and Other Incredibly Critical People* (Oakland: New Harbinger, 2012), 36.

21. Lucy M. Kim, Judith L. Johnson, and Jennifer Ripley, "A 'Perfect' Storm: Perfectionism, Forgiveness, and Marital Satisfaction," *Individual Differences Research* 9, no. 4 (2011): 199–209.

22. Lionel Adey, *Hymns and the Christian Myth* (Vancouver: University of British Columbia Press, 1986), 84.

23. Gary Chapman, *The Marriage You've Always Wanted* (Chicago: Moody, 2009), 29.

24. C. Samuel Storms, *To Love Mercy: Becoming a Person of Compassion, Acceptance, and Forgiveness* (Colorado Springs: NavPress, 1991), 44–45.

25. Brené Brown, *The Gifts of Imperfection: Let Go of Who You Think You're Supposed to Be and Embrace Who You Are* (Center City, MN: Hazelden, 2010), 56.

26. Wendell Berry, *The Unsettling of America: Culture and Agriculture* (San Francisco: Sierra Club, 1977), 222.

27. Scot McKnight, *The Jesus Creed: Loving God, Loving Others* (Brewster, MA: Paraclete, 2004), 83.

28. Eugene H. Peterson, *Five Smooth Stones for Pastoral Work* (Grand Rapids: Eerdmans, 1980), 95.

29. Robert C. Shippey Jr., *Listening in a Loud World: Toward a Theology of Meaning* (Macon, GA: Mercer University Press, 2005), 85.

30. See Gal. 5:22–23.

31. Michael Jackson, *Moonwalk* (New York: Random House, 1988), 184.

32. Dietrich Bonhoeffer, *Creation and Fall: A Theological Interpretation of Genesis 1–3* (New York: Macmillan, 1959), 27.

33. Bruce C. Birch, *To Love as We Are Loved: The Bible and Relationships* (Nashville: Abingdon, 1992), 26.

34. Stephen M. Haas and Laura Stafford, "Maintenance Behaviors in Same-Sex and Marital Relationships: A Matched Sample Comparison," *The Journal of Family Communication* 5, no. 1 (2005): 43–63.

35. Sharon Jayson, "Married Couples Who Play Together Stay Together," *USA Today*, July 15, 2008, http://usatoday30.usatoday.com/news/nation/2008-07-15-fun-in-marriage_N.htm.

36. Eugene H. Peterson, *A Long Obedience in the Same Direction: Discipleship in an Instant Society* (Downers Grove, IL: InterVarsity, 1980), 159.

37. 2 Cor. 12:9.

38. Henri J. M. Nouwen, *Clowning in Rome: Reflections on Solitude, Celibacy, Prayer, and Contemplation* (New York: Doubleday, 1979), 3.

39. Michael E. McCollough, Paul Orsulak, Anna Brandon, and Linda Akers, "Rumination, Fear, and Cortisol: An In Vivo Study of Interpersonal Transgressions," *Health Psychology* 26, no. 1 (February 2007): 127.

40. Sara LaBelle, Melanie Booth-Butterfield, and Keith Weber, "Humorous Communication and Its Effectiveness in Coping with Interpersonal Transgressions," *Communication Research Reports* 30, no. 3 (2013): 221–29.

41. Shannon M. Maki, Melanie Booth-Butterfield, and Audra McMullen, "Does Our Humor Affect Us? An Examination of a Dyad's Humor Orientation," *Communication Quarterly* 60, no. 5 (2012): 649–64.

42. James M. Houston, *I Believe in the Creator* (Grand Rapids: Eerdmans, 1980), 219.

Chapter 4 Know Yourself

1. Joe Queenan, "The Fall of the Workplace Jerk," *Wall Street Journal*, July 2, 2009, A13.

2. See, e.g., Ron Welch, *The Controlling Husband: What Every Woman Needs to Know* (Grand Rapids: Revell, 2014).

3. Matt. 7:3–5.

4. The ideas of cocooning and criticizing developed in this chapter are loosely based on the concepts of *hiding* and *hurling* found in J. Grant Howard, *The Trauma of Transparency: A Biblical Approach to Inter-Personal Communication* (Portland, OR: Multnomah, 1979).

5. Matt. 18:15–17.

6. Taking excessive credit for successes and abdicating responsibility for failures is referred to as *self-serving attribution bias*. For work on attribution theory and research, see Valerie L. Manusov and John H. Harvey, eds., *Attribution, Communication Behavior, and Close Relationships* (Cambridge, MA: Cambridge University Press, 2001).

7. Arthur L. Cantos, Peter H. Neidig, and K. D. O'Leary, "Men and Women's Attributions of Blame for Domestic Violence," *Journal of Family Violence* 8, no. 4 (1993): 289–302.

8. Cornelius Plantinga Jr., *Not the Way It's Supposed to Be: A Breviary of Sin* (Grand Rapids: Eerdmans, 1995).

9. Prov. 27:19.

10. See Sarah Trenholm and Arthur Jensen, *Interpersonal Communication*, 7th ed. (New York: Oxford University Press, 2013), 9–14.

11. The idea that humans misorder even good desires (misordered desires/loves is "cupidity") has a long history in philosophy and theology but is generally credited to Augustine of Hippo, who saw sin not just in terms of transgressions against God and neighbor but also in terms of human beings' tendency not to follow the order of the law of love, particularly by failing to love God above all other loves. See, e.g., Paula Fredriksen, *Sin: The Early History of an Idea* (Princeton: Princeton University Press, 2012), 125.

12. See Julia T. Wood, *Communication in Our Lives*, 6th ed. (Boston: Wadsworth, 2012), 11.

13. The idea of human communication as action is ancient, but in the twentieth century it was associated primarily with speech-act theory first developed at length by British philosopher J. L. Austin. See, e.g., J. L. Austin, *How to Do Things with Words*, 2nd ed., ed. J. O. Urmson and Marina Sbisà (Cambridge, MA: Harvard University Press, 1975). For an explicitly Christian application of speech-act theory, see Nicholas Wolterstorff, *Divine Discourse: Philosophical Reflections on the Claim That God Speaks* (Cambridge, MA: Cambridge University Press, 1975).

14. Susan Donaldson James, "Immigrant Teen Taunted by Cyberbullies Hangs Herself," *ABC News*, January 26, 2012, par. 3, http://abcnews.go.com/Health/cyber-bullying-factor-suicide-massachusetts-teen-irish-immigrant/story?id=9660938.

15. John Maxwell, *Everyone Communicates, Few Connect: What the Most Effective People Do Differently* (Nashville: Nelson, 2010), 3.

16. An *imagined interaction* is partly the process of imagining—thinking through—how one might respond in anticipation of an interpersonal encounter or of reliving an interaction to evaluate how one might have acted differently. See James M. Honeycutt, "Imagined Interaction Theory: Mental Representations of Interpersonal Communication," in *Engaging Theories in Interpersonal Communication: Multiple Perspectives*, ed. Leslie A. Baxter and Dawn O. Braithwaite (Thousand Oaks, CA: Sage), 77–87.

17. Brennan Manning, *Abba's Child: The Cry of the Heart for Intimate Belonging* (Colorado Springs: NavPress, 2002), 161.

18. Ibid., 20.

19. Minsun Shim, Joseph N. Cappella, and Jeong Yeob Han, "How Does Insightful and Emotional Disclosure Bring Potential Health Benefits? Study Based on Online Support Groups for Women with Breast Cancer," *Journal of Communication* 61, no. 3 (June 2011): 448.

20. Caroline J. Simon, *The Disciplined Heart: Love, Destiny, and Imagination* (Grand Rapids: Eerdmans, 1997), 28.

Chapter 5 Relate Openly

1. Susan Tardanico, "Is Social Media Sabotaging Real Communication?," *Forbes*, April 30, 2012, http://www.forbes.com/sites/susantardanico/2012/04/30/is-social-media-sabotaging-real-communication.

2. Katy Baumbach, G. L. Forward, and David Hart, "Communication and Parental Influence on Late Adolescent Spirituality," *Journal of Communication and Religion* 29, no. 2 (2006): 393–420; G. L. Forward, Alison Sansom-Livolsi, and Jordanna McGovern, "College Student Communication, Religiosity, and Family Satisfaction: The Importance of Opposite-Sex Parent Relationships," *Journal of Communication and Religion* 31, no. 2 (2008): 245–71.

3. James 3:4–5.

4. Eugene H. Peterson, *Traveling Light: Modern Meditations on St. Paul's Letter of Freedom* (Colorado Springs: Helmers & Howard, 1988), 50.

5. D. W. Winnicott, "Ego Distortion in Terms of True and False Self," in *The Maturational Process and the Facilitating Environment: Studies in the Theory of Emotional Development* (New York: International Universities Press, 1965), 140–52.

6. Ni Preston, "Can Less Time on Facebook Increase Your Happiness? Yes! The Emotional Price of Comparing with Others on Facebook," *Psychology Today*, August 11, 2013, http://www.psychologytoday.com/blog/communication-success/201308/can-less-time-facebook-increase-your-happiness-yes.

7. Pope Benedict XVI, "Truth, Proclamation and Authenticity of Life in the Digital Age," message for the 45th World Communications Day, June 5, 2011, http://www.vatican.va/holy_father/benedict_xvi/messages/communications/documents/hf_ben-xvi_mes_20110124_45th-world-communications-day_en.html.

8. Stephanie Davenport, "How Could He Lie to Me? I'd Never Keep Secrets from Him. Would I?," *Marriage Partnership*, September 2008, http://www.kyria.com/topics/marriagefamily/marriage/communication/16.14.html.

9. Connie Cass, "Americans Losing Trust in Each Other, Poll Finds," *Monterey Herald*, November 30, 2013, http://www.montereyherald.com/news/ci_24630614/americans-losing-trust-each-other-poll-finds.

10. The question of intention, although tricky and debated, is generally present but not required for an Augustinian understanding of a lie; for a thorough explication of Augustine's views of a lie, see Paul J. Griffiths, *Lying: An Augustinian Theory of Duplicity* (Grand Rapids: Brazos, 2004).

11. Marilyn Chandler McEntyre, *Caring for Words in a Culture of Lies* (Grand Rapids: Eerdmans, 2009), 42.

12. Sissela Bok, *Lying: Moral Choice in Public and Private Life* (New York: Vintage, 1979), 61.

13. David P. Gushee, "The Truth about Deceit: Most Lies Are Pitiful Attempts to Protect Our Pride," *Christianity Today*, March 2006, 68.

14. Sean M. Horan and Melanie Booth-Butterfield, "Is It Worth Lying For? Physiological and Emotional Implications of Recalling Deceptive Affection," *Human Communication Research* 37, no. 1 (2011): 78–106.

15. Ronny E. Turner, Charles Edgley, and Glen Olmstead, "Information Control in Conversations: Honesty Is Not Always the Best Policy," *Kansas Journal of Sociology* 11, no. 1 (1975): 69–89.

16. Carl Camden, Michael T. Motley, and Ann Wilson, "White Lies in Interpersonal Communication: A Taxonomy and Preliminary Investigation of Social Motivations," *Western Journal of Communication* 48, no. 4 (1984): 309–25.

17. Bianca Beersma and Gerben A. Van Kleef, "Why People Gossip: An Empirical Analysis of Social Motives, Antecedents, and Consequences," *Journal of Applied Social Psychology* 42, no. 11 (2012): 2640–70.

18. Tim Stafford, *That's Not What I Meant!* (Grand Rapids: Zondervan, 1995), 91.

19. R. T. Kendall, *Controlling the Tongue* (Lake Mary, FL: Charisma House, 2007), 168.

20. Adapted from Matthew Feinberg, Robb Willer, Jennifer Stellar, and Dacher Keltner, "The Virtues of Gossip: Reputational Information Sharing as Prosocial Behavior," *Journal of Personality and Social Psychology* 102, no. 5 (2012): 1015–30.

21. Stafford, *That's Not What I Meant!*, 92.

22. Marsha Dutton, *Aelred of Rievaulx: The Historical Works*, trans. Jane Patricia Freeland (Kalamazoo, MI: Cistercian, 2005), 93.

23. Prov. 11:13.

24. C. S. Lewis, *Mere Christianity* (New York: Simon & Schuster, 1996), 79.

25. Bok, *Lying*, 136.

26. H. Paul Grice, "Logic and Conversation," in *Studies in the Way of Words*, ed. H. P. Grice (Cambridge, MA: Harvard University Press, 1989), 22–40.

27. John Powell, *Why Am I Afraid to Tell You Who I Am?* (Niles, IL: Argus, 1969), 12.

28. Paul A. Soukup, *Out of Eden: Seven Ways God Restores Blocked Communication* (Boston: Pauline Books & Media, 2006), 37.

29. Robert E. Fisher, *The Language of Love: Spiritual Guidelines for Communication* (Cleveland, TN: Pathway, 1987), 55.

30. Stafford, *That's Not What I Meant!*, 50.

31. Sarah Sumner, "The Seven Levels of Lying: We Lie More Than We Think. And That's Part of the Problem," *Christianity Today*, May 20, 2011, http://www.christianitytoday.com/ct/2011/may/7-levelslying.html.

32. Scot McKnight, *The Jesus Creed: Loving God, Loving Others* (Brewster, MA: Paraclete, 2004), 70.

33. Fisher, *Language of Love*, 55.

34. O. S. Hawkins, *Tearing Down Walls and Building Bridges* (Nashville: Nelson, 1995), 151.

35. Gushee, "Truth about Deceit," 68.

Chapter 6 Encourage Others

1. *Pursuit of Happyness*, directed by Gabriele Muccino (2006; Culver City, CA: Columbia Pictures, 2007), DVD.

2. Russell Baker, *Growing Up* (New York: Signet, 2004), 239.

3. Job 5:7.

4. Rodney A. Reynolds, "Discouraging Messages," *Communication Reports* 19, no. 1 (2006): 16–30.

5. Cited in John C. Maxwell, *Encouragement Changes Everything* (Nashville: Nelson, 2008), 19.

6. 1 Cor. 16:13; Eph. 6:10; 1 Cor. 1:7.

7. Eph. 1:11.

8. See, e.g., 1 Thess. 5:9–11.

9. 1 Thess. 5:14; John 11:19, 31.

10. Kathleen Ellis, "Perceived Parental Confirmation: Development and Validation of an Instrument," *Southern Communication Journal* 67 (2002): 319–24.

11. Paul Schrodt, Andrew M. Ledbetter, and Jennifer K. Ohrt, "Parental Confirmation and Affection as Mediators of Family Communication Patterns and Children's Mental Well-Being," *Journal of Family Communication* 7, no. 1 (2007): 23–46.

12. Rene M. Dailey, "Confirmation in Parent-Adolescent Relationships and Adolescent Openness: Toward Extending Confirmation Theory," *Communication Monographs* 73, no. 4 (2006): 434–48.

13. Heb. 10:24–25.

14. E.g., "First, I thank my God through Jesus Christ for all of you, because your faith is being reported all over the world" (Rom. 1:8). "I always thank my God for you because of his grace given you in Christ Jesus" (1 Cor. 1:4).

15. Acts 18:27.

16. Acts 4:36–37.

17. Acts 9:27.

18. Acts 15:36–40.

19. Diane Disney Miller, "My Dad, Walt Disney," *Saturday Evening Post*, November 17, 1956, 30.

20. Aristotle, *Rhetoric*, trans. W. Rhys Roberts (New York: GoodTimes, 2014), 7.

21. Sam Crabtree, *Practicing Affirmation: God-Centered Praise of Those Who Are Not God* (Wheaton: Crossway, 2011), 22.

22. James 3:7–9.

23. Crabtree, *Practicing Affirmation*, 33.

24. Max De Pree, *Called to Serve: Creating and Nurturing the Effective Volunteer Board* (Grand Rapids: Eerdmans, 2001), 66–67.

25. Ian M. Tait, "Calvin's Ministry of Encouragement," *Presbyterian* 11, no. 1 (Spring 1985): 99.

26. O. S. Hawkins, *Tearing Down Walls and Building Bridges* (Nashville: Nelson, 1995), 44.

27. C. Samuel Storms, *To Love Mercy: Becoming a Person of Compassion, Acceptance, and Forgiveness* (Colorado Springs: NavPress, 1991), 120.

28. Wendy L. Watson, *Rock Solid Relationships: Strengthening Personal Relationships with Wisdom from the Scriptures* (Salt Lake City: Deseret, 2003), 30.

29. Larry Crabb and Dan Allender, *Encouragement: The Key to Caring* (Grand Rapids: Zondervan, 1984), 91.

30. Paul Moots, *Becoming Barnabas: The Ministry of Encouragement* (Herndon, VA: Alban Institute, 2004), 7.

31. Jack Zenger and Joseph Folkman, "The Ideal Praise-to-Criticism Ratio," *Harvard Business Review*, March 15, 2013, http://blogs.hbr.org/2013/03/the-ideal-praise-to-criticism/.

32. R. T. Kendall, *Controlling the Tongue* (Lake Mary, FL: Charisma House, 2007), 172.

33. Crabb and Allender, *Encouragement*, 121.

34. Ps. 34:18.

35. Ps. 147:3.

Chapter 7 Promote Peace

1. Amanda Lee Myers and Christine Armario, "Love Is Gone, but Marriage Survives," *Grand Rapids Press*, December 14, 2008, A18.

2. C. Samuel Storms, *To Love Mercy: Becoming a Person of Compassion, Acceptance, and Forgiveness* (Colorado Springs: NavPress, 1991), 116.

3. Kristen L. Johnson and Michael Roloff, "Serial Arguing and Relational Quality," *Communication Research* 25, no. 3 (1998): 327–43.

4. Kathryn Dindia, "Definitions and Perspectives on Relational Maintenance Communication," in *Maintaining Relationships through Communication: Relational, Contextual, and Cultural Variations*, ed. Daniel J. Canary and Marianne Dainton (Mahwah, NJ: Erlbaum), 1–28.

5. Duane Elmer, *Cross-Cultural Conflict: Building Relationships for Effective Ministry* (Downers Grove, IL: InterVarsity, 1993), 29.

6. Katheryn C. Maguire and Terry A. Kinney, "When Distance Is Problematic: Communication, Coping, and Relationship Satisfaction in Female College Students' Long-Distance Dating Relationships," *Journal of Applied Communication Research* 38, no. 1 (2010): 27–46.

7. Katheryn C. Maguire, "Bridging the Great Divide: An Examination of the Relationship Maintenance of Couples Separated by War," *Ohio Communication Journal* 45 (2007): 131–58.

8. Richard Kraut, *What Is Good and Why: The Ethics of Well-Being* (Cambridge, MA: Harvard University Press, 2007), 161.

9. Jard DeVille, *Pastor's Handbook on Interpersonal Relationships: Keys to Successful Leadership* (Grand Rapids: Baker, 1986), 194.

10. Richard Lischer, *The End of Words: The Language of Reconciliation in a Culture of Violence* (Grand Rapids: Eerdmans, 2005), 149.

11. See, for instance, William R. Lovallo, *Stress and Health: Biological and Psychological Interactions*, 2nd ed. (Thousand Oaks, CA: Sage, 2004).

12. Adapted from Tim Muehlhoff, *I Beg to Differ: Navigating Difficult Conversations with Truth and Love* (Downers Grove, IL: InterVarsity, 2014), 51–53.

13. Ibid., 51.

14. Sue Shellenbarger, "Advances in Couples Therapy Tackle Trauma of Infidelity," *Wall Street Journal*, November 12, 2008, D1.

15. Gershen Kaufman, *Shame: The Power of Caring*, 2nd ed. (Cambridge, MA: Schenkman, 1985), 21.

16. Abraham J. Heschel, *Who Is Man?* (Stanford, CA: Stanford University Press, 1965), 81–82.

17. Ibid., 46–47.

18. Martin Buber, *I and Thou* (New York: Scribner, 2000). Also see Nick J. Watson, "Martin Buber's I and Thou: Implications for Christian Psychotherapy," *Journal of Psychology and Christianity* 25, no. 1 (2006): 34–43.

19. Eugene H. Peterson, *A Long Obedience in the Same Direction: Discipleship in an Instant Society* (Downers Grove, IL: InterVarsity, 2000), 52.

20. Frederick Buechner, *Wishful Thinking: A Seeker's ABC*, rev. ed. (San Francisco: HarperOne, 1993), 25.

21. Corey L. M. Keyes and Jonathan Haidt, "Introduction: Human Flourishing—The Study of That Which Makes Life Worthwhile," in *Flourishing: Positive Psychology and the Life Well-Lived*, ed. Corey L. M. Keyes and Jonathan Haidt (Washington, DC: American Psychological Association, 2003), 6.

22. Bruce C. Birch, *To Love as We Are Loved: The Bible and Relationships* (Nashville: Abingdon, 1992), 67.

23. Exod. 21:23–24; Matt. 5:38–39.

24. Matt. 5:38–39.

25. Paul David Tripp, *War of Words: Getting to the Heart of Your Communication Struggles* (Phillipsburg, NJ: P&R, 2000), 110.

26. Ps. 133:1.

27. Ken Sande, *The Peacemaker: A Biblical Guide to Resolving Personal Conflict*, 3rd ed. (Grand Rapids: Baker Books, 2004), 46.

28. Isa. 11:6; 65:25.

29. Rom. 12:18.

30. Sande, *Peacemaker*, 44; see Luke 1:79; cf. Isa. 2:2–4.

31. Prov. 16:7.

32. Kraut, *What Is Good and Why*, 5.

33. Ps. 52:8–9.

34. Kenneth Burke, *A Rhetoric of Motives* (Berkeley: University of California Press, 1969), quoted in Jeffrey W. Murray, *Kenneth Burke: A Dialogue of Motives* (Lanham, MD: University Press of America, 2002), 102.

35. Michael D. Sedler, *When to Speak Up and When to Shut Up* (Grand Rapids: Chosen, 2003), 34.

36. Leslie A. Baxter, "A Dialectical Perspective on Communication Strategies in Relationships Development," in *A Handbook of Personal Relationships*, ed. Steve Duck (New York: Wiley, 1988), 257–73.

37. Saul Lieberman, quoted in Elie Wiesel, *And the Sea Is Never Full: Memoirs, 1969–*, trans. Marion Wiesel (New York: Knopf, 1999), 130.

38. R. T. Kendall, *Controlling the Tongue* (Lake Mary, FL: Charisma House, 2007), 33.

39. Allan Wade, "Small Acts of Living: Everyday Resistance to Violence and Other Forms of Oppression," *Contemporary Family Therapy* 19, no. 1 (March 1997): 23.

40. Lewis B. Smedes, *Forgive and Forget: Heal the Hurts We Don't Deserve* (New York: HarperCollins, 1996), 139.

41. Prov. 15:1.

42. Matt. 5:5.

43. Tim Stafford, *That's Not What I Meant!* (Grand Rapids: Zondervan, 1995), 45.

44. Col. 4:6; Eph. 4:29; also see Robert E. Fisher, *The Language of Love: Spiritual Guidelines for Communication* (Cleveland, TN: Pathway, 1987), 81.

45. Stanley Hauerwas, interview by Tamara Jaffe-Notier, "An Iconoclast Looks at the Cross-Shattered Christ," *The Wittenburg Door*, September/October 2006, 19.

46. Prov. 14:16.

47. Walter J. Ong, SJ, *The Presence of the Word: Some Prolegomena for Cultural and Religious History* (New Haven: Yale University Press, 1967), 192.

48. Lew Vander Meer, *Recovering from Churchism: How to Renew, Grow, and Celebrate Your Church* (Grand Rapids: Edenridge, 2012), 36.

49. Gal. 3:28.

50. Elmer, *Cross-Cultural Conflict*, 29.

Chapter 8 Restore Relationships

1. Joyce Vissell and Barry Vissell, "A Father's Apology to His Son," http://www.support4change.com/index.php?option=com_content&view=article&id=137:fathers-apology-to-his-son.

2. R. T. Kendall, *Total Forgiveness* (Lake Mary, FL: Charisma House, 2007), 13.

3. Alexander Pope, *Essay on Criticism*, line 525, paraphrased in Pope, *Essay on Criticism*, ed. Alfred S. West (Cambridge: Cambridge University Press, 2014), 57.

4. The decision to discuss granting forgiveness prior to seeking and accepting forgiveness is based on the fact that the literature has focused predominately on ways to help us extend forgiveness to others, with much less attention to the importance of recognizing our need for forgiveness or how to graciously accept forgiveness from others. See Fraser Watts, "Christian Theology," in *Forgiveness in Context: Theology and Psychology in Creative Dialogue*, ed. Fraser Watts and Liz Gulliford (New York: T&T Clark, 2004), 59–60. Psychological approaches to forgiveness center primarily on how the victim grants forgiveness to the offender, whereas religious views focus on seeking and accepting forgiveness. See Jesse Couenhoven, "Forgiveness and Restoration: A Theological Exploration," *Journal of Religion* 90, no. 2 (2010): 160.

5. Ken Sande, *The Peacemaker: A Biblical Guide to Resolving Personal Conflict*, 3rd ed. (Grand Rapids: Baker Books, 2004), 207.

6. C. S. Lewis, *The Weight of Glory* (San Francisco: HarperOne, 2009), 182.

7. Luke 10:37.

8. See the definition of forgiveness in Robert D. Enright, Suzanne Freedman, and Julio Rique, "The Psychology of Interpersonal Forgiveness," in *Exploring Forgiveness*, ed. Robert D. Enright and Joanna North (Madison: University of Wisconsin Press, 1998), 46–47.

9. Matt. 18:22.

10. Eph. 4:32.

11. Watts, "Christian Theology," 58.

12. J. K. Rowling, *Harry Potter and the Half-Blood Prince* (New York: Scholastic, 2005), 96.

13. Kendall, *Total Forgiveness*, 37.

14. Ken Sande with Tom Raabe, *Peacemaking for Families: A Biblical Guide to Managing Conflict in Your Home* (Wheaton: Tyndale, 2002).

15. Kendall, *Total Forgiveness*, 75.

16. Lewis B. Smedes, *Forgive and Forget: Heal the Hurts We Don't Deserve* (New York: HarperCollins, 1996), 29.

17. Ron Welch, "Four Ways to Fail at Forgiving Your Spouse," *Crosswalk.com*, August 13, 2014, http://www.crosswalk.com/family/marriage/engagement-newlyweds/4-ways-to-fail-at-forgiving-your-spouse.html.

18. Smedes, *Forgive and Forget*, 39.

19. Fred Luskin, *Forgive for Love: The Missing Ingredient for a Healthy and Lasting Relationship* (New York: HarperCollins, 2007), 23.

20. William Paul Young, *The Shack: Where Tragedy Confronts Eternity* (Newbury Park, CA: Windblown, 2007), 224.

21. Renee Coates Scheidt, "Wrestling with a Broken Heart," *Just between Us*, http://www.justbetweenus.org/pages/page.asp?page_id=88013.

22. Tim Muehlhoff and Todd V. Lewis, *Authentic Communication: Christian Speech Engaging Culture* (Downers Grove, IL: InterVarsity, 2010), 124.

23. Charles Gibson, "Amish Say They 'Forgive' School Shooter," *ABC News*, October 3, 2006, http://abcnews.go.com/WNT/Story?id=2523941.

24. Avis Clendenen and Troy Martin, *Forgiveness: Finding Freedom through Reconciliation* (New York: Crossword, 2002), 15.

25. Robert K. Cheong and Frederick A. DiBlasio, "Christ-Like Love and Forgiveness: A Biblical Foundation for Counseling Practice," *Journal of Psychology and Christianity* 26, no. 1 (2007): 22.

26. Clendenen and Martin, *Forgiveness*, 6.

27. Scot McKnight, *The Jesus Creed: Loving God, Loving Others* (Brewster, MA: Paraclete, 2004), 70.

28. Chris R. Morse and Sandra Metts, "Situational and Communicative Predictors of Forgiveness Following a Relational Transgression," *Western Journal of Communication* 75, no. 3 (2011): 239–58.

29. Vincent R. Waldron and Douglas L. Kelley, *Communicating Forgiveness* (Thousand Oaks, CA: Sage, 2008), 147.

30. Douglas L. Kelley and Vincent R. Waldron, "An Investigation of Forgiveness-Seeking: Communication and Relational Outcomes," *Communication Quarterly* 53, no. 3 (2005): 339–58.

31. Frederick A. DiBlasio, "Christ-like Forgiveness in Marital Counseling: A Clinical Follow-up of Two Empirical Studies," *Journal of Psychology and Christianity* 29, no. 4 (2010): 291–300.

32. Charles L. Griswold, *Forgiveness: A Philosophical Exploration* (Cambridge: Cambridge University Press, 2007), 122.

33. Loren L. Toussaint and David R. Williams, "National Survey Results for Protestant, Catholic, and Nonreligious Experiences of Seeking Forgiveness and of Forgiveness of Self, of Others, and by God," *Journal of Psychology and Christianity* 27, no. 2 (2008): 120–30.

Conclusion Celebrate Friendships

1. C. S. Lewis, *The Four Loves* (New York: Harcourt, 1960), 96–97.

2. Ibid., 169.

3. C. S. Lewis, *God in the Dock* (Grand Rapids: Eerdmans, 1970), 49.

4. C. S. Lewis, *The Problem of Pain* (New York: Macmillan, 1962), 93.

5. Albert M. Wolters, *Creation Regained: Biblical Basics for a Reformational Worldview*, 2nd ed. (Grand Rapids: Eerdmans, 2005), 44.

6. Rom. 16:16; 1 Cor. 16:20; 2 Cor. 13:12; 1 Thess. 5:26.

7. Lewis, *Four Loves*, 84.

Index